"In this excellent work, Dr. and the competency of wha disciling and counseling the deeper hurts and sinful failings of the soul. This book is a must-read for any Christian who desires to disciple and counsel others, especially pastors, elders, and church leaders. It is a gold mine of insight!"

John D. Street, Chair, Graduate Department of Biblical Counseling, The Master's University & Seminary

"Dale Johnson is a gift to the church, as is this book. I highly recommend it for all who strive for a richer understanding of local church ministry and all who are committed to biblical approaches to pastoral care and Christian community."

Jason K. Allen, President, Midwestern Baptist Theological Seminary & Spurgeon College

"This book is a positive and biblical encouragement for local churches to fulfill their privilege and responsibility to serve struggling men and women with truth from God's sufficient Word. Readers will see Christ exalted as his church is given the position of prominence in soul-care that his precious blood purchased for our good and his glory."

Steve Viars, Faith Church and Biblical Counseling Ministry, Lafayette, IN

"With a pastor's heart and clear biblical teaching, Dale Johnson clarifies the characteristics of a church that does soul care well. Pastors will find this book essential for fine-tuning their own vision, useful for leadership training, and helpful for Sunday school classes and small group discussions."

Jim Berg, ACBC and ABC Certified Biblical Counselor; council member, Biblical Counseling Coalition; professor of biblical counseling, Bob Jones University Seminary; author of *Changed into His Image* and *Quieting a Noisy Soul*; founder of Freedom That Lasts

"Johnson has met a true need with this book and very appropriately issues a clarion call for a more excellent way to care for one another within the church. A scholar and former pastor himself, he has a clear passion to encourage leaders within the church to build a culture of care consistent with Jesus and his Word, for his glory and the sake of his body, the church."

Stuart W. Scott, Professor of Biblical Counseling, The Master's University, Santa Clarita, CA; director of membership services, the Association of Certified Biblical Counselors (ACBC)

"Dale Johnson presents God's design and intention for the church as the context for real nurture and growth through biblical care and counseling. This volume is a treasure chest full of ecclesiological wisdom conveyed in practical instruction for both leaders and laity. I'll be asking our whole church body to read and apply it!"

Rick Holland, Senior Pastor, Mission Road Bible Church, Prairie Village, KS

"As God's household, the church of Jesus Christ is the pillar and foundation of God's truth, yet the modern church has neglected its role to biblically counsel its members. Against this backdrop, Dale Johnson asserts a simple, timely, compelling claim: God has called the church to be a culture of care. Gratefully, Johnson captures the Bible's vision and provides direction for how church leaders and church members should fulfill it."

Robert D. Jones, Biblical Counseling Professor, The Southern Baptist Theological Seminary; author of *Pursuing Peace, Uprooting Anger,* and coauthor of *The Gospel for Disordered Lives*

"Dale Johnson writes a timely and needed primer on the role of the church in the care of souls. This reminder comes with gentle exhortations, informed critiques, and humble clarifications. Moreover, it provides a biblically informed call to action for the church of Jesus Christ. As a pastor and a missionary, I am thrilled for this much-needed resource to be in the hands of church members, pastors, and seminarians."

Juan F. Moncayo, Senior Pastor, Iglesia La Fuente, Quito, Ecuador

"This book makes the brilliant move to aim at the whole culture of a church—its shared beliefs and values, which will shape its practices far more effectively than any policy change ever could. Care should seem normal in the church because it is at the heart of Jesus's ministry."

Jeremy Pierre, Lawrence & Charlotte Hoover Professor of Biblical Counseling, The Southern Baptist Theological Seminary; author of *The Dynamic Heart in Daily Life*

"'The church is God's agent to care for the souls of his people.' That's a game-changer statement that needs to impact the church. Dale has done a great job writing about a much-needed topic in a clear, biblical, loving, and accurate way. With clear and key definitions, examples, and essential theological concepts for every believer, this is a must-read for every believer to know and be challenged to obey God's Word to care for one another.

Kike Torres, Lead Pastor, Horizonte, Queretaro, Mexico; ACBC Certified member; president of the Biblical Counseling Coalition Mexico; author of *A New Life*

"The church is the arena in which we enjoy the love of God triune. One of the chief ways we express and experience this love is in caring for one another. In this volume, Dr. Dale Johnson provides a timely reminder of this truth, along with an insightful analysis of what it means for the church to cultivate a culture of care. Here is a rich resource for all believers, whether they be in the pulpit or the pew."

J. Stephen Yuille, Vice President of Academics, Heritage College & Seminary; associate professor of Biblical Spirituality, The Southern Baptist Theological Seminary

The Church as a Culture of Care

Finding Hope in Biblical Community

T. DALE JOHNSON JR.

New
Growth
Press
newgrowthpress.com

New Growth Press, Greensboro, NC 27401
newgrowthpress.com

Cover Design: Ben Stafford, www.benillustrated.com
Interior Design and Typesetting: Gretchen Logterman

ISBN: 978-1-64507-182-2(Print)
ISBN: 978-1-64507-183-9 (eBook)

Library of Congress Cataloging-in-Publication Data
Names: Johnson, T. Dale, author.
Title: The church as a culture of care : finding hope in biblical
community
/ T. Dale Johnson, Jr.
Description: Greensboro, NC : New Growth Press, [2021] | Includes
bibliographical references and index. | Summary: "Biblical counselor
Dale Johnson explains that the church is still the primary place where
those who struggle can receive lasting hope and healing"-- Provided by
publisher.
Identifiers: LCCN 2021033367 (print) | LCCN 2021033368 (ebook) |
ISBN 9781645071822 (print) | ISBN 9781645071839 (ebook)
Subjects: LCSH: Caring--Religious aspects--Christianity. |
Communities--Religious aspects--Christianity. | Mission of the church.
Classification: LCC BV4647.S9 J64 2021 (print) | LCC BV4647.S9
(ebook) | DDC 262--dc23
LC record available at https://lccn.loc.gov/2021033367
LC ebook record available at https://lccn.loc.gov/2021033368

Printed in the United States of America

28 27 26 25 24 23 22 21   1 2 3 4 5

To my parents, Tommy Dale and Nancy Johnson,
who taught me to fear the Lord and love others,
especially those who are of the household of faith.

Contents

Introduction

Many years ago, as a sophomore in college, I decided to major in psychology. I believed that God was calling me to serve in pastoral ministry, and I thought studying psychology would help me understand how to help people. But even as a young Christian, I had many reservations about my psychology courses. The theories of Freud, Rogers, and others seemed inconsistent with a biblical understanding of people and their problems. At the same time psychology was intriguing, even fascinating, to study. I remember thinking things like *oh, so that's why we act like that,* or *this is why my family does things that way.* The study of psychology was beginning to shape my foundational thinking about humanity, but I struggled to square it with what the Bible clearly taught to be true about people.

During this time, I had a casual lunch meeting with a local pastor. I had not intended to discuss my concerns with him, but we ended spending most of our time talking about the psychology courses I was taking. He began to shed light on my experience by explaining how the underlying ideology and primary tenets of modern psychology were in direct competition with Scripture. He recommended that I read an author named Jay Adams and said that he would be a refreshing voice to a young man like me who wanted to know and understand how to help people from a biblical perspective.

I took his advice and started to read everything that Adams—who most would call the father of biblical counseling—had written. It was like having a light bulb come on in my head as he defended the place of soul care in the church and the primacy of Scripture in that care. His work articulated many of the concerns I had and also gave me a road map for a truly Christian counseling ministry under the authority of the church, dependent upon the Scripture and the work of the Holy Spirit.

Adams once said that a definitive work or two needed to be written on the role of the church in soul care and counseling. This book is my attempt to respond to the need Dr. Adams recognized, but it is in no way an attempt to write something "definitive." I am sure after reading you will agree that more needs to be done. However, my goal is to help Christians begin to recover the necessity of the church for soul care. I hope this book will encourage healthy discussion that will allow the church, and the Scripture entrusted to her, to be central to the conversation regarding soul care.

Another reason I am writing this book is that Christians who have sought to integrate the Bible with secular psychology have often claimed that the Bible does not offer specific techniques or methods for the counseling task and is, therefore, insufficient. Their approach to soul care attempts to blend secular psychology with theology. Their argument is that the Bible does not speak about the modern problems described by mental health and psychiatry. While they are careful not to dismiss the Bible's usefulness in total, they say it is only sufficient and authoritative for a small section of people's needs that are *spiritual*. They argue that psychology is given to us by means of common grace or general revelation and is authoritative and sufficient to address the broadening psychological aspects of humanity. They point out that the Bible is not a scientific textbook, doesn't have comprehensive or exhaustive information about human-kind, and does not provide a methodology for counseling.

While I agree the Bible is not intended to be a "textbook" in the style we think of such resources today, their perspective dismisses the validity of God's purpose for the church and the God-given functions of the church for the task of soul care. My goal is to help us unpack the way God has equipped his people for every function of the church as an integral part of the care of souls. God has provided the church with the necessary resources and design for us to care well for one another with the Word of God, by the power of the Holy Spirit, as we are led by Christ.

The Bible does not provide the kind of methodological approach to soul care that appeases behavioral scientists, because the Bible reveals a different perspective on people and their struggles than the popular therapeutic philoso-phies. They claim the Bible is insufficient for soul care because it is not an exhaustive resource. But if we are to measure counseling psychologies and mental health by that same standard—the need to have exhaustive information in order to be useful—then we will not find sufficient help there either. The Bible does, however, present a comprehen-sive approach to soul care where Jesus is at the center of restoration (although he will never fit neatly within the para-digm of counseling psychologies). It's that biblical approach to soul care that we will begin to explore in this book.

A third purpose of the book is to challenge the current narrative which dismisses the church as an antiquated or unprepared institution for the care of souls. Many claim that prayer is too simplistic, the Word of God too antiquated, and the Holy Spirit insufficient to help the broken and the needy. But Christians too easily dismiss God's supernatural resources and his church as a vital means of God's intended care for disquieted souls. The dismissal of these resources graciously provided to us by our all-sufficient God leaves us dependent upon the insufficient and ever-shifting shadows of earthly wisdom. It has always been difficult for me to understand how many who claim that God's resources are insufficient are willing to put so much trust and faith in human resources like modern psychology—a subjective, limited, constantly changing, and nonexhaustive explanation for human problems.

I realize that churches are full of sinners, who can and do sin against each other. Far too many churches have a culture that has harbored or hidden the carnage of sin, instead of being a haven of restoration from sin's destruction. But that doesn't mean we should dismiss the necessity of the church. Instead, we need to repent and return to the purposes and design God established in order to see true restoration.

This book is intended to be an admission of our failures and an exhortation to arise and reclaim the church as a culture of care. Interwoven in the discussion will be critiques on ideas that have hindered the church, admissions of our abdications in deference to the cultural tides of care, and a call to reconsider the beauty and intention of God's church as the institution responsible to restore the brokenhearted back to the fullness of life abundant in Christ, who restores the soul.

My hope and prayer is that this book is one of the means God uses to spur churches and their leaders to grow more faithful in living out their call to provide care for souls. The church is best positioned and equipped to bear the burden of soul care. God has not given any other institution the responsibility to minister to the problems of life. Every counseling system attempts to offer a worldview to answer meaningful human questions. If we believe in the authority and sufficiency of God's Word, we are convinced that the Christian worldview provides the true foundation and clearest lens for us to understand the problems of the human soul.

So many of the troubles we face in life are vexations of the soul as we wrestle with the realities of our own mortality, purpose, meaning, and value. God has given his church the responsibility to steward souls by providing context for our human experiences and hope for true restoration in Christ. The Bible explains our human experiences better than any human wisdom. May we be found faithful to love as Christ, shepherd as Christ, care as Christ, and mend the brokenhearted as Christ, to the praise of his glory.

CHAPTER ONE

Whose Job Is Soul Care?

Suppose a young man—let's call him Sam—came to you because his life had disintegrated. He described a series of sad events that had left him desperate. His wife Aisha had left him, taking Jerome, their baby boy, with her. He had lost his job. He felt all alone in the world and passed his time playing video games and drinking too much. You know he needs help, but who can help? Are his problems relational? Is his drinking an addiction with a physical basis? Why can't he hold down a job? Of course, it's possible that he should see a medical doctor, maybe a lawyer, or even someone to help him find another job, but where should he start?

Start with the Church

God's Word tells us to start with his church. That's what this book is about—reclaiming the church as God's agent to care for the souls of his people—people like Sam and Aisha. The Scripture paints a picture of the world as full of consistently desperate and broken people, who are in constant need of and dependent upon God's care. The New Testament traces for us how the early church cared for those whose lives were overcome with grief, lust, anger, selfish ambition, and a host of other problems. Some troubles were caused by personal sin, and others by suffering in a world cursed by sin. Nevertheless, the apostle Paul consistently reminded believers of the benefits of God's Word, the fellowship of the saints, and the power and presence of the Holy Spirit as means of comfort and correction to the weary, wounded, or wayward soul (2 Corinthians 1:37; 1 Thessalonians 4:18).

From its inception, the church has been a constant, although never perfect, haven for the downcast and hurting. For centuries, the church was the first place that people would turn for help with their inner anguish. Gregory the Great's *The Book of Pastoral Rule* encouraged a focus on shepherding and tender care for church leaders in the sixth century. A book compiled by Theodore Tappert, *Luther's Letters of Spiritual Counsel*, catalogs several of the constant inquiries Martin Luther received for spiritual counsel and his attempts at biblical soul care. Luther's student Martin Bucer wrote the well-known work *Concerning the True Care of Souls*, in which Bucer used Ezekiel 34 as a model of pastoral care. He assumed that the responsibility of care was the burden of the church carried primarily by pastors. The Puritans certainly added to the notion that the church, particularly her leaders, were responsible to shepherd the flock of God through their soulish vexations. This is how pastors became known as physicians of the soul.

But today the church is not usually the first place, or even the second place, people turn to for help with their troubles. Sometimes the church is viewed so negatively that it's not even the last resort. As Jerry Bridges remarked, "There is a crisis of caring in the Church of Jesus Christ today."[1] There are a variety of reasons for this, including broader cultural shifts and the fact that the church has not always been a good steward of its responsibility to provide soul care. Often we in the church have ostracized sinners and added to the burdens of sufferers. And yet, God has called the church and equipped her with sufficient resources to care for the sinner and sufferer alike. For these failures, both past and present, we must repent of our blindness and our neglect toward caring for others the way God intended—as his hands and feet.

We also must consider how entrenched modern culture's assumption is that secular, professionalized counseling provides the template by which all counseling approaches should be measured. The modern secular paradigm has become so dominant that it has often clouded the minds of believers to the vitality of the Scripture and the design of God's church for the ministry of soul care. Many modern Christians view the paradigm of counseling and soul care from a secular perspective, and dismiss the Bible because it does not seem to have an equivalent structure, methods, or techniques that fit the mold of secular counseling models. So, some Christians have neglected the Scriptures altogether for soul care—giving that essential church function to secular professionals. Other Christians, who don't want to throw the Scripture away entirely, have worked to incorporate the Bible within established secular systems of care. This school of thought, which we will call "integrationism," often has good intentions, but does not see the primacy of the Bible for soul care. An unintended consequence is the continued professionalism of soul care, the neglect of the Scripture, and the marginalization of the church's role to care for souls.

A Definition of Biblical Counseling and Purpose

Unlike secular counseling, biblical counseling doesn't stand alone. The very name "biblical counseling" points to the truth that, at its core, biblical counseling has no grounding without the Scripture and no authority outside of the church of Jesus Christ. God has given his church the responsibility and calling to minister the Scripture so the broken can be healed and the lost saved. To do the personal ministry work of biblical counseling is to do the mission and ministry of the church.

How do we faithfully respond to God's call and, by the power of the Holy Spirit, renew the church as a culture of care?

Let's begin by defining biblical counseling. Biblical counseling, as a modern movement, began more than fifty years ago with the publication of Jay Adams's seminal work, *Competent to Counsel.*[2] Since then, the biblical counseling movement has continued to grow and is now in its third generation.[3] With the growth of any movement, it is always helpful to revisit key tenets. Dr. Samuel Stephens, my colleague at Midwestern Baptist Theological Seminary, and I co-wrote the following definition to offer a starting point for understanding biblical counseling's foundations, parameters, and goals:

> Biblical counseling is the personal discipleship ministry of God's people to others under the oversight of God's church, dependent upon the authority and sufficiency of God's Word through the work of the Holy Spirit. Biblical counseling seeks to reorient disordered desires, affections, thoughts, behaviors, and worship toward a God-designed anthropology in an effort to restore people to a right fellowship with God and others. This is accomplished by speaking the truth in love and applying Scripture to the need of the moment by comforting the suffering and calling sinners to repentance, thus working to make them mature as they abide in Jesus Christ.

Dr. Stephens and I plan to write a series of works in the future that explore the different elements of the definition above. This book will touch on several aspects of this definition, but its primary purpose is to explain the importance of the clause "under the oversight of God's church," and to present a theologically grounded vision of the church as a culture of care.

The Church Is Responsible for the Care of Souls

Who is responsible for the care of souls? There are a wide variety of approaches to answering this question. We might try to identify who we believe does soul care *best*. We may answer based on our experiences, and then decide who should be responsible from the data we gather. While this approach may yield valuable insights, it should not be how we, as Christians, engage such a question.

As Christians, our priorities demand that we consider the question from the position of Scripture first. Has God granted one of his ordained institutions the authority and responsibility to provide soul care? As John MacArthur said, "A truly *Christian* worldview . . . is one in which the Word of God, rightly understood, is firmly established as both the foundation and the final authority for everything we hold true."[4] Those who do not believe the Bible is God's revelation will certainly have a different approach to answering this question. Understandably, they begin with a variety of presuppositions that help them create meaning from observable data in the world. For Christians, however, the Scriptures must be the lens through which we see the world. The Bible is not the only place where Christians should seek information, but it must be the first place we go to understand the data we observe and the last place we go to make sense of it in God's world. Otherwise, the data we observe will be ordered in earthly terms and constructs which will cloud our understanding of people and their problems in God's world and ultimately send us in the wrong direction to find solutions.

God-Ordained Institutions

Who has been given the responsibility to carry God's message of care and restoration? Who has God given the responsibility to demonstrate the care of Christ for the broken? Who is to be the hands and feet of the Lord Jesus to bind up the brokenhearted?

We will begin this part of the discussion within the context of the doctrine of jurisdiction. The doctrine of jurisdiction—or as some have called it, "sphere sovereignty"—simply acknowledges that God in his infinite wisdom has established legitimate earthly authorities for his glory and our good.[5] Setting this parameter assumes that God is sovereign, and that he has ordained certain institutions with responsibilities in the social order. Most of the time this discussion is scaled down to speak of these institutions in terms of civil authorities (state), family, and church.[6]

Self-governance is an important truth—we will all, individually, be held accountable to God for our thoughts and deeds (Romans 14:10–12). Yet, there is a danger in limiting our view only to individual accountability. Instead, we need to see that all of life is under God's jurisdiction and that therefore we will be held to account by him for the way we act toward others and toward his established institutions. Francis Schaeffer said, "the Lordship of Christ covers all of life and all of life equally. It is not only that true spirituality covers all of life, but it covers all parts of the spectrum of life equally. In this sense there is nothing concerning reality that is not spiritual."[7] In contrast to our culture which encourages individual choice based on our own thoughts, feelings, and desires, it is important to note that we honor the Lord by our submission to legitimate authorities.

The authority given to these distinct entities is a stewardship with roles and responsibilities. Each of God's ordained institutions will give an account for how their God-given responsibilities are stewarded for his name and for his purposes. The authority granted is only delegated and is not ultimate—God is the only sovereign.

Government

Ruling authorities bear a solemn and civil duty for which they will give an account to God. It is always important to keep the authority of the government within proper perspective. "God has ordained the state as a delegated authority," Schaeffer said, "it is not autonomous."[8] God is sovereign and this is his world. He reigns over all things and all things are subject to him. God entrusts the government with a certain role and responsibility to steward within the social order. We acknowledge that this is a good thing. and as Christians we are commanded to obey the ruling authorities. By that obedience, we honor God (Romans 13).

As with every human institution, governing authorities are not always righteous and, at times, are difficult to obey. As believers, however, we are called to pray for the ones who lead. We are called to obey unless they require compliance against the commands of God. The ruling authorities—whether we call them kings, governors, or presidents—are appointed by God. Whether the process be democratic or not, it is God's sovereign hand which oversees the ascendency to those positions of power (Daniel

2:21). God may use some rulers as a blessing to his people, and he may use some to discipline or judge. As believers, we must remain steadfast in our obedience to God in the way we obey the ruling authorities, knowing that God will hold them accountable for their stewardship of authority—whether good or evil (1 Peter 2:13–23).

Of course, this does not mean that we are called to blindly obey ruling authorities. Schaeffer again reminds us, "If there is no place for civil disobedience, then the government has been made autonomous, and as such, it has been put in the place of the Living God."[9] For those who trust in Jesus, God is our highest authority. His commands are not to be compromised. If an earthly ruler, being evil, requires us to breach a command of God or our clear conscience to obey him as sovereign, then we must be courageous to disobey and say as Peter did, "We must obey God rather than men" (Acts 5:29).

That does not mean we have a license to disobey the government at any point that we simply disagree. Rather in those cases, our disagreements with the acts of government should drive us to our knees to pray for those who have authority over us. We are to pray for them so that we can live quiet and peaceable lives and for the sake of gospel proclamation (1 Timothy 2:2–3).

The primary point I want to make here is that the government is not responsible for the care of souls. They have a purpose in God's world, and we are to pray for our governing officials. We are to comply with governing authorities when they are not requiring us to disobey God. The reason I make this distinction is that many Christians live as if the government, by regulation and licensing of individuals who practice counseling, is primarily responsible for the domain of soul care. Yet, that is not the primary role given for which our governing officials will give an account to God.

Church

In the same way that it is not the government's responsibility to oversee the care of souls, it is not the church's responsibility to punish through incarceration or other physical means those who do evil. The church is not responsible to be God's "avenger who carries out God's wrath on the wrongdoer"; that is the role of the governing authorities that "have been instituted by God" (Romans 13:1–4). The church is responsible, however, for the care of souls. In most every function of the church described in Scripture, the care of souls is a primary aim (Galatians 6:1–2; 2 Timothy 4:1–5; James 5:13–16).

The biblical counseling movement has consistently given responsibility to the church as the God-ordained institution to offer his care to the broken. God has entrusted his means of grace through the Word and the Spirit in the work of the church to heal the brokenhearted (Ezekiel 34:16ff). As the statement from the Association of Certified Biblical Counselors says, the church "is the main agent for all ministry of the Word, including the ministry of counseling and discipleship."[10]

This has been biblical counseling's focus from its inception. "Counseling is the work of the Holy Spirit," Adams said. "Effective counseling," he continued, "cannot be done apart from him."[11] In more definitive terms Adams said, "The authority for counseling is granted through Christ's Church."[12] David Powlison agreed: "Biblical-nouthetic counseling was initiated to provide two things: a cogent critique of secularism and a distinctly biblical alternative." Powlison provided further clarification by adding, "Biblical counseling operates within the worldview of the Bible, with Bible in hand. It is centered on God even (especially!) when it thinks about man. It is centered on Jesus Christ, who became a man in order to save us. It is centered in the midst of Christ's people who are called to pray for one another and to counsel one another in love."[13] Heath Lambert, a third-generation biblical counselor, reiterated that foundational presupposition when he began his theology book with the statement, "Counseling is a theological discipline."[14] He added, "If counseling is grounded in our understanding of the truth, and the truth is rightly upheld in the context of the church, then counseling finds a real home in the church."[15]

It makes sense that those who don't believe in the authority of Scripture would question and argue against this perspective. As Christians, we clearly possess distinct beliefs about the realities of life. But these should not be controversial statements when a person believes basic Christian doctrines. From a Christian worldview, counseling is a theological discipline based upon the Word of God and the work of the Spirit of God. Biblical counseling is centered upon Jesus's finished work which enables us to change from the inside out, love one another, and walk in peace amid the chaos caused by sin and suffering. If that is the case, then it seems reasonable to say that the church is the institution God has made responsible for the care of souls.

While primary streams of the biblical counseling movement have remained consistent in their declaration of the church's responsibility for soul care, they are only a supporting opinion. The real question is, what does God's Word say about the burden of responsibility for the care of souls? The answer to that question provides our starting point for how we build a system of soul care.

The Church Responsible

As has been clearly articulated by several, the church in the modern world is experiencing a crisis of direction.[16] The church seems to consistently wrestle with how to be relevant for a modern audience. While much has been written on this subject, often the discussions tend to center around various functions of the church. These are important discussions, but many begin with pragmatic assumptions—as if the church is free to operate any way we choose to accomplish the purposes we want. Even when we have good and godly end goals, this pragmatic approach proves detrimental in accomplishing God's purposes for the church. We could address the many ways this has negatively affected the church, but for our purposes, I would like us to consider the detriment that has occurred to our practice of soul care.

The Bible teaches that the church is responsible to God to steward the duties and authority he has given to us. The church, with Christ as its head, has been granted authority in the sphere of the human soul, by which to redeem, restore, heal, cleanse, and grow in purity—in a nutshell, to care for souls. We can see how God cares for the souls of his people all through the Bible, beginning with his gracious care for Adam and Eve in the garden. His care can be seen in the favor Noah found, in the deliverance secured in Moses, and the blessing of Abraham. We can see God's care in the promised Messiah, who would come as the Prince of Peace and Wonderful Counselor of Isaiah 9:6, and the Great Shepherd who would heal the brokenhearted in Ezekiel 34:11–16. God is the one who cares, and a primary aim of the Old Testament is that care would come to fruition in the person of Jesus Christ.

Jesus demonstrated this care toward the sinners he encountered and in his death for sinners like us. The words of Jesus, the Good Shepherd, provide a sense of his commission to the church to care for the broken. "Go therefore and make disciples of all nations, baptizing them in the name of the Father and of the Son and of the Holy Spirit, teaching them to observe all that I have commanded you" (Matthew 28:19–20). Discipleship is God's primary means of restoring his people because discipleship is the intentional pursuit of becoming conformed to the image of Christ.

In the name of Jesus, salvation is found, sins are forgiven, hearts are made new, the wounded and broken are healed, we are changed into his image, and humanity is made whole. The work of the church is to care for souls in clear proclamation of the name and gospel of Jesus. No other entity can accomplish the work God requires of his church, by his Word, through the power of the Holy Spirit. Jesus is the balm in Gilead to heal the wounded soul and the true bread of heaven to sustain us.

Every aspect of the work of the church is intended to care for souls. Preaching, shepherding, one-anothering, church discipline, missionary proclamation, personal obedience—all are intended to awaken or strengthen the soul to live faithfully and peacefully in a war-torn and sin-cursed world. If Jesus cared for others by the truth of God's Word in these various ways, shouldn't the church under his headship do the same without reservation?

We can see our responsibility as a church in the tasks given to leaders to keep watch over our souls (Hebrews 13:17). The call of the "one anothers" in the New Testament is another clear evidence that the church, under the headship of Christ, is to care for souls by making everyone complete in Christ (Colossians 1:28). In the chapters that follow I will offer key passages from Scripture, identify cultural influences to avoid, and then present critical facets of the church as God's primary means of applying Christ as the one who cares for and restores the souls of humanity.

Before we embark on a close examination of why and how the church has failed to care for souls, the next chapter will present a positive vision of what it looks like for a church to have a "culture of care." This is not meant to be a cookie-cutter formula that can be used to replicate a culture of care in your church. Rather, it is meant to bring clarity to the characteristics of a church that does soul care well and to serve as a challenge to revisit God's design of the church and her functions as his method of caring for all of our human weaknesses.

Discussion Questions

1. How does this chapter challenge or change the way you think about the church's role in "soul care"?

2. What roadblocks do you see in your own church to becoming the primary way that souls are cared for? What would you have to change? What are you already doing to care for souls?

3. If Sam came to your church for help, what would he find? Does your pastor have the primary responsibility for helping Sam? What (or who) else might be helpful to him?

Chapter Two

A Biblical Vision for the Church as a Culture of Care

Cultures are built upon conventional wisdom formed by accepted values, shared beliefs, common practices, and prevailing goals. Different places in different times in history had distinct cultures that guided life on a day-to-day basis. As I have traveled, it is very apparent that there are differing values and practices than I was accustomed to growing up in the southeastern portion of the United States. I have noticed even in the midwestern part of the US, where I live now, folks talk a little differently (they have the accent, not me!), use variations of slang, have different family traditions, and other minor distinctions that create slightly different elements to the culture. Sometimes we describe these distinctions by different cuisines, different customs, different languages, or different styles of living. In Christian ministry, we even train missionaries to be aware of "culture shock" as they prepare to enter a country different from their own.

Church Culture

Churches also have a culture of their own. Do you remember the "worship wars" of several years ago, when churches would bicker over the contemporary or traditional forms of singing during the worship service? Behind those struggles were different ideas about what the culture of the church should be. Many things are part of building the culture of a church. It might be the location of the building, the setting of the stage, the type of pulpit the preacher uses, or the order of the service. The church may be known for its preaching or music. A church may be known for its outreach or the community involvement. All of these elements contribute to the culture of the church. Any outsider coming into a church will sooner or later realize what the culture of your church is. It's what you will be known for to the outside world.

The culture that grows within a church does not happen accidentally. Culture is a fostered entity among a fellowship of believers. And once culture is established, it can be hard to change. Trying to change the culture of a church can be a significant and difficult task for even the most seasoned elders and leaders. There are so many things that can contribute to church culture, but Jesus tells us the most important thing that the church should be known for. He said in John 13:34–35, "A new commandment I give to you, that you love one another; just as I have loved you, you also are to love one another. By this all people will know that you are my disciples, if you have love for one another."

Are we known by the way in which we care for one another? We are known for all sorts of things, but this one particular demand of Christ seems to slip by as an optional piece of the values, behaviors, and goals which should shape our interactions among the fellowship of brothers and sisters. While we may critique one another for various preferences with how we do church (sometimes rightfully so), we must not forget that one of the primary ways we are to be known is as a family of people who deeply love and care for one another.

We can be a church that has sound preaching and theologically accurate worship, but without this type of love and care for one another we are a clanging symbol to each other and the world. The culture of our church is important because it conveys, intended or not, what we value as a body of believers. We may disagree over some of the particulars of how the church should function, but one thing that is nonnegotiable is that we should be a people known as disciples of the Lord Jesus because of the way we love and care for one another.

The Church as a Culture of Care

Care Is Natural

Caring is an instinctive response to hurting and pain. The human desire to care can be viewed as a common grace of God. Even those we consider most vile have companions within their inner circle for whom they demonstrate care and concern. This is not to say that the way in which evil people offer care is unaffected by sin, but simply that the instinct to care for those hurting is as natural as falling asleep after the sun sets.

Take, for example, a man with the hardest of hearts, and watch him hold his firstborn child. In a way that little else can, his newborn can melt his rigid heart. He will fight anyone or anything that would attempt to cause harm to his little child. His instinct is to care for and protect his child.

Do you recall when you taught your children to ride their bike? You carefully guided them down the driveway or across the yard, holding tightly to the back of their seat and running as fast as your aged legs would move. The thrill of riding was worth the risk of their falling, but you kept special care to keep them from that scrapped knee or stitched head. If they began to fall, you did everything in your power to catch them, to protect them, to care for them.

Offering care, even if for somewhat selfish purposes, is as common as a reflex. It is no wonder then that the secular culture attempts to offer care to those who hurt. As much as I critique the secular philosophies behind many counseling theories, the desire to offer care usually come from a heart that wants to help someone who is vulnerable, needy, and/ or hurt.

Distinctions of Care

One area of common ground that Christians share with unbelievers is that we experience pain. We share health challenges, disappointments, emotional distresses, and even death. Yet, the Bible indicates that believers deal with those losses differently than the world. Paul reminds us that we do not have to "grieve as others do who have no hope" (1 Thessalonians 4:13). We acknowledge that Christians share in all of the sufferings, weaknesses, and inadequacies common to all of humanity. What we disagree over is *why* we have those experiences, *how* we should describe those experiences, and *what* we should do about them.

As Christians we believe that the problems of this world are rooted in humanity's rebellion against a holy God. Our whole being—the inner and outer person—suffers tremendously due to the results of human sin. Christians must not live divorced from these scriptural truths. That is not a denial of our problems, but the correct context to explain the root of the various problems we have as fallen human beings. This is the broad biblical answer to why we struggle. If we leave out a proper doctrine of sin in our explanations of the primary causes of human problems, then we tend to describe those experiences in secular terms.

Why is it so important to use biblical categories in describing human problems? Because when we describe our problems using secular categories and labels, we tend to seek the solutions provided by secular wisdom. If our problems are due to the effects of the fall, there is always hope for us. We can turn to Christ who promises to make all things new. In Christ, the hardest struggles of life—whether from our own sins or the suffering that comes from living in a sin-broken world, can be redeemed. But if we rely on secular labels and the solutions that are attached to them, our hope will rise and fall upon the temporary effectiveness of those solutions.

Secular categories of describing human problems come in a myriad of forms that range from Freudian fixation, Skinnerian animalistic instincts, to Rogerian incongruence, and beyond. Those explanations have evolved to include the lack of self-esteem, genetic causation, and many others. While problems are no different in the way humans experience them, secular psychological theory does not consider supernatural realities. Therefore, they explain the experiences of people as produced by other types of forces or influences. Problems are reduced to psychological or biological problems.

Noting the fundamental difference in approach between the Bible and secular psychology does not mean that I am advocating a hyper-spiritual perspective that ignores physical issues. We will discuss this in more depth in chapter three, "When the Church Doesn't Care," but for now it's important to note that the Bible teaches that every human is body and soul, material and immaterial. We have soulish problems, and we have physical ailments. However, there is not a radical division between the soul and the body. Instead, the Bible teaches us that we are embodied souls.

The two worlds, physical and spiritual, are both present in our human nature and are virtually inseparable, except by death. Christians should refrain from reducing problems to spiritual-only issues, but neither should we make the same mistake with physical maladies. If we do, we err in our understanding of biblical anthropology. When we redefine our human problems into "psychological-only" or "biological-only" categories, we validate secular thinking and become susceptible to their humanly devised but empty solutions.

We believe that Jesus was sent not only to save us from our sins but also to empower us by the Holy Spirit to live a holy life, no matter what circumstances we face. This extension of the purpose for which Christ came enables us to recognize that all of life is to be lived under the lordship of Jesus. This perspective erases the dichotomy between *spiritual* issues and *nonspiritual* issues. In God's economy, all issues are under his lordship, and facing them is an opportunity to turn to him for the help we need.

Biblical Considerations

Every aspect of the work of the church is intended for the glory of God and to care for souls. I will provide a more in-depth discussion of how each of the functions of the church is a form of soul care in chapter six, "The Care of Christ's Under-Shepherds," and chapter seven, "Equipping the Saints."

In this section we will briefly consider several critical Scripture texts which help to unpack how the church is intended to be a distinct culture of care. I have already mentioned Jesus's statement in John 13:35, "By this all people will know that you are my disciples, if you have love for one another." We are called to love each other deeply the same way Christ loves us. Christ's love for us is not merely reciprocal love, which has little cost attached to it. Instead, the love with which Christ says we are to love one another is a demonstrative, sacrificial love. This is not a natural type of love in a sin-cursed world, but it can become so among believers in the church because Christ has redeemed us and made us new. He has loved us first, so we can pour out his love from our hearts to others.

The way that the New Testament describes pastoral work demonstrates that the church is the means that God uses to pour out his love in care for sinners and sufferers. Consider the following passages:

> Pay careful attention to yourselves and to all the flock, in which the Holy Spirit has made you overseers, to care for the church of God, which he obtained with his own blood. (Acts 20:28)

> Is anyone among you suffering? Let him pray. Is anyone cheerful? Let him sing praise. Is anyone among you sick? Let him call for the elders of the church, and let them pray over him, anointing him with oil in the name of the Lord. And the prayer of faith will save the one who is sick, and the Lord will raise him up. And if he has committed sins, he will be forgiven. Therefore, confess your sins to one another and pray for one another, that you may be healed. The prayer of a righteous person has great power as it is working. (James 5:13–16)

> And he gave the apostles, the prophets, the evangelists, the shepherds and teachers, to equip the saints for the work of ministry, for building up the body of Christ, until we all attain to the unity of the faith and of the knowledge of the Son of God, to mature manhood, to the measure of the stature of the fullness of

Christ, so that we may no longer be children, tossed
to and fro by the waves and carried about by every
wind of doctrine, by human cunning, by craftiness
in deceitful schemes. Rather, speaking the truth in
love, we are to grow up in every way into him who
is the head, into Christ, from whom the whole body,
joined and held together by every joint with which
it is equipped, when each part is working properly,
makes the body grow so that it builds itself up in
love. (Ephesians 4:11–16)

Him we proclaim, warning everyone and teaching everyone with all wisdom, that we may present
everyone mature in Christ. (Colossians 1:28)

But we will devote ourselves to prayer and the ministry of the word. (Acts 6:4)

All this is from God, who through Christ reconciled us to himself and gave us the ministry of reconciliation; that is, in Christ God was reconciling
the world to himself, not counting their trespasses
against them, and entrusting to us the message of
reconciliation. Therefore, we are ambassadors for
Christ, God making his appeal through us. We
implore you on behalf of Christ, be reconciled to
God. (2 Corinthians 5:18–20)

Obey your leaders and submit to them, for they are
keeping watch over your souls, as those who will
have to give an account. Let them do this with joy
and not with groaning, for that would be of no
advantage to you. (Hebrews 13:17)

Even this brief listing of a few relevant texts points to the care of souls as the church's responsibility. Pastors are called and responsible to care for the souls of God's flock. They are to do this through prayer and ministry of the Word so that sinners will be reconciled to God and saints will be matured and helped. They are to do this with joy because they will give an account to God for this most important work. To drive this point home even further, the next few sections will explain three of the primary reasons why the church should provide care for souls.

We Care Because He First Cared for Us

The reason why the church is *able* to provide care for the souls of the lost, hurting, and wayward is because God first cared for us. He is the source, strength, and demonstration of true love and care. As 1 John 4:19 says, "We love because he first loved us." As mentioned earlier, we can see God's gracious care beginning in the garden. His provision of Eve for Adam after acknowledging that he was alone, plants bearing food to sustain them, and means to commune with him, are a few of the ways God provided intimate care. Perhaps the best display of God's care came when our first parents sinned against him, and he sought them out and covered their guilt and shame with the shed blood of an animal. God's care in the garden introduced the world to his grace, even for those who acted as his enemies. It was in the garden at that tender and shameful moment that the Father unveiled his character as absolutely holy, yet filled with mercy. Along with judgment for sin, he announced the Beloved who would come from the seed of woman to care for his people (Genesis 3:16). As the revelation of God unfolds, the clarity and intention of his care is explained as Immanuel, God with us—realized in Jesus—God in the flesh. His care can be most fully seen in the person of Jesus Christ when he gave his life as a ransom, shed his blood to atone for our sins, and provided his righteousness to cover our shame.

Even as Jesus faced death, he cared for his disciples by telling them he would not "leave [them] as orphans" (John 14:18). His promise to come to his disciples was fulfilled at Pentecost when the Spirit filled his people—convicting, comforting, and empowering them just as Jesus had promised (John 14:16). Today Jesus cares for his people in the very same way—through his Spirit who dwells in us, filling us with the love of Christ and empowering us to turn from sin and turn toward Jesus for forgiveness and help in our time of need.

Receiving care from the Holy Spirit feeds our souls and provides us with the strength needed to do battle with our sin and find refuge in him in the midst of suffering. And yet, disciples of Jesus should not just be recipients of care; we are called to be caregivers. Ephesians 5:1 says that we are to be "imitators of God, as beloved children." This call to imitate God's compassionate care is made even more explicit in 2 Corinthians 1:4, which says that God "comforts us in all our affliction, so that we may be able to comfort those who are in any affliction, with the comfort with which we ourselves are comforted by God." We care *because* he first cared for us.

We Care Because It Is for His Glory

Another reason why God has commissioned the church to provide care for souls is because it brings glory to him. As Jesus said in Matthew 5:16, "In the same way, let your light shine before others, so that they may see your good works and give glory to your Father who is in heaven." The church is responsible to God for the care of souls because in fulfilling this responsibility, the church brings glory to God.

No other institution is commissioned by God to accomplish this great work.

Over and over again in the Scriptures we see that God is zealous for his own glory, and Christians are called to the same zeal. First Peter 2:11–12 reminds us "to abstain from the passions of the flesh, which wage war against your soul. Keep your conduct among the Gentiles honorable, so that when they speak against you as evildoers, they may see your good deeds and glorify God on the day of visitation." Peter continued to motivate us to work for the glory of God, "whoever speaks, as on who speaks oracles of God; whoever serves, as on who serves by the strength that God supplies—in order that in everything God may be glorified through Jesus Christ" (1 Peter 4:11).

We Care Because It Is for Our Good

The primary reason we care for others is out of our love for God, but another reason why the church should provide soul care is because it is for our good. One of the main ways that God works in the world in these last days is through the words and deeds of the church. Repeatedly in the New Testament the church is called "the body of Christ." And while we certainly must care for the souls of the lost who are currently outside of the church, there is also a clear call for the various members of the body of Christ to nurture and support the other members (Galatians 6:10). The call of the "one another" commands in the New Testament provide clear evidence that the church, under the headship of Christ, is to make everyone complete in Christ. Do not miss the critical point that all of the work of becoming complete in Christ is soul care. This type of mutual care for one another makes us vulnerable to others and helps us to live in a way that promotes dependence on him. We express our dependency on Christ by also accepting and depending on help from the family of God. Instead of self-sufficiency, we learn together Christ-sufficiency.

We were made to depend on God and each other. As Christians, we are called to pour ourselves into the care of others. When we do, we experience the pleasure of God. Living this way fills us with true satisfaction and blessing. The Psalmist declared, "Behold how good and pleasant it is when brothers dwell in unity!" (Psalm 133:1). Remember Paul's exhortation to the Ephesian elders: "In all things I have shown you that by working hard in this way we must help the weak and remember the words of the Lord Jesus, how he himself said, 'It is more blessed to give than receive'" (Acts 20:35).

Christlike Care Is Supernatural

The biblical counseling view of soul care is that it requires dependence upon the supernatural resources provided by God. This is a difficult, faith-building and faith-challenging truth. By contrast, most counseling psychologies can be refined down to two distinct issues. First, they are attempting to describe true human change outside of God's process of sanctification. Second, each counseling psychology proposes some sort of means for insight into the inner workings of the human soul that is a replacement for the work of the Holy Spirit described in Scripture.

As human beings in our modern age, this type of dependence is uncomfortable. We would rather be dependent upon some strength within ourselves or some system we can master and manipulate to offer some form of help. Our scientific age constantly forces us to consider ways that our abilities or intellect may overcome some human ailment. The reality is that we do not have anything that we did not receive (1 Corinthians 4:7). We are dependent upon God for everything, so we should not be surprised that Christlike care is supernatural. Dependence upon supernatural resources is uncomfortable because it makes our human weaknesses more evident, but this allows us to glory in our weakness so that Christ is made strong (2 Corinthians 12:9). Contrary to what we might think, embracing our weaknesses is not bad. Being dependent upon a good, loving, kind, faithful, gracious, infinite, all-powerful, all-knowing, and merciful God for our care is much more hopeful than depending upon the shifting shadows of this temporal world (James 1:17). The fact that God invites us to join his work in the "one anothers" of Scripture—to love, serve, and minister the Word to each other—is both an amazing privilege and a daunting responsibility. In fact, it is a responsibility that can't be taken on without the power and the presence of the Holy Spirit.

Saying that Christlike care is supernatural does not mean that there is nothing we can do in the process of care. It simply means that we are fully dependent upon the work of God to enlighten, convict, change, comfort, and keep an individual. Christlike care produces lasting hope and lasting change into the image of Christ and that is a work that only God can do by the power of his Spirit and through the Word in the hearts of people.

What Is Normal?

Finally, I want to demonstrate that not only has God uniquely called the church to provide soul care, but he has also provided the church with something the world cannot offer: an objectively true picture of what it means to be "normal." This is an important consideration for at least two reasons.

First, it is for the glory of God that Christ came to save sinners. He lived perfectly to demonstrate a life that was devoted fully to God. Jesus is certainly exemplary for us as human beings, but he is much more than that. Second, one of the primary reasons we are called as believers to be conformed to the image of Christ is because he lived as humanity was intended to live. Jesus demonstrates what healthy humanity was to live like, reflecting the character of God and living fully dependent upon him. As a part of our restoration, we are changed from one degree of glory to another as we are conformed to the image of Christ (Romans 8:29; 2 Corinthians 3:18). While in one sense Jesus is a far cry from normal as the God-man, in another sense he expresses the true measure of what normal human life was intended to be like in submission and honor to the Father (Ephesians 4:13–16).

Have you considered what it means to be normal? That is an odd question and tough to answer. Consider the varieties of people in the world. We share many things in common, but when you begin to describe things that are *normal* it is not as easy a task as you might think. The key is having some sort of basis or foundation which describes or exemplifies what is intended to be normal behaviors, emotions, attitudes, or passions.

The *Diagnostic and Statistical Manual of Mental Disorders* (*DSM*) has been the secular guidebook since the 1950s for understanding human psychological abnormality. Over time, the book has grown in size and influence within our culture. At one time the book was only utilized in psychiatric care to help practitioners use a common language to describe the ailments of various patients. Now, however, the book is viewed as the "Bible" of psychiatry. Rather than a book that leads to the promised land, it is a book that leads to a barren land providing more questions about our human condition than answers of hope. The *DSM* offers hundreds of diagnoses to categorize abnormal human behaviors and emotions, all without ever defining normal human experience.

For Christians, this ought to be a somewhat alarming revelation, or at least raise a yellow flag of caution. How do we define abnormal states of human experience without first having some sort of understanding of normalcy? It seems as though the *DSM* begins with a cultural appraisal of normalcy, and then on the basis of this ever-shifting understanding proceeds to describe unwanted emotions and behaviors as "abnormal." But how do we measure normal versus abnormal? Are we simply describing unwanted behaviors and emotions or are the diagnoses genuinely abnormal? Are these descriptions bound to a western cultural context or are these universal human abnormalities? For humans, what does it mean to be normal?

Jesus Is Normal

Secular systems rely on descriptions that accurately describe our experiences, but they fail to put those experiences in context. The lack of a true definition of "normal" also contributes to a struggle to recognize what normal suffering looks like versus a threshold that crosses over into abnormality.

Christianity is different; we have an objective basis for defining what it means to be normal when it comes to human experience. Theologians have often described Jesus as the "true human."[1] As Mark Jones said, "There is nothing in us that was lost that Christ did not save. Therefore, the eternal Son had to take into union with himself a complete human nature so that we might one day know what it really means to be human, completely restored in the image of God without defilement."[2] This statement, of course, does not take away from his divinity. Jesus was and is fully God. Yet in Christian orthodoxy, we also believe Jesus came to earth as fully human. As the second Adam, he lived life as humanity was designed by God to live. Jesus lived fully dependent upon the Father, reflecting the character of God in true worship and communion with him, while pouring himself out in love toward others and living in communion with them.

As Heath Lambert says,

> Everything we need from God requires us to trust in Jesus to receive it. Jesus's sinlessness makes him distinct from every other human being, but that does not make him less human. Indeed, the lack of sin in Jesus makes him *more* human than any other person. You do not have to sin in order to be human. Far from it. In fact, human beings were not designed to sin. They were created to glorify God with all of who they are. Sin, as it warps our design to honor God, actually dehumanizes us. Jesus' sinless perfection—far from minimizing his full humanity—actually maximizes it. We will not realize the full potential of our own humanity until we are free from the scourge of sin.[3]

Thus, we recognize what is normal and abnormal based upon seeing how Jesus lived his life. The secular culture has no such way to delineate "normal"; therefore they struggle to categorize what is abnormal. But we can define normal humanity according to Jesus. Christianity has an aim, a focus: that we be conformed to his image. This implies that in our natural state, we are abnormal. It is an assumption that we need change, we need help, and we are desperately dependent upon God to fulfill our true God-given purpose. This is why Jesus is central to soul care.

We will further unpack this idea of what is truly "normal" and how Jesus shepherds us back to wholeness, in chapter five, "Christ as Our Good Shepherd." But for now, let's remember that the church is how Jesus shepherds our souls as we hear the counsel of God, through his Word and by the Holy Spirit. In the church, Jesus himself mends, encourages, comforts, heals, and restores us. He is our Shepherd. He guides us gently as we are conformed to his image. It is in him we return back to health, back to normal for the glory of God and the good of our hearts. The church has been entrusted with the truth that conforms us to the image of God by the work of the Spirit. So we guard, defend, and proclaim the truth in order to make disciples who are restored from broken, blind, and self-exalting to clearer and clearer images of the peaceful and stable character of God.

Conclusion

Even though the church is responsible for the care of souls, that does not mean she always performs that stewardship well. Even when the church does not fulfill her responsibility to care for souls in a God-honoring way, that does not change the fact that the church is responsible for the care of souls. Our primary posture must be to obey those who are in authority over us in the church so long as those in authority are not requesting obedience that is contrary to God's commands. As with any human institution ordained by God, we are only commanded to obey "in the Lord" (Ephesians 6:1). Those of us who have been hurt by the church may take comfort in the knowledge that the leaders of the church will be held accountable for how they have stewarded their responsibility before God (Hebrews 13:17). Further discussion of how to respond to and seek healing from real harm done by the church is outside the scope of this book.[4] However, since the primary audience of this book is church leaders, the following chapter will explore some of the main reasons why the church fails to care well, and will drive home the importance of taking this responsibility seriously by describing some of the consequences of the church's failure in this area.

Discussion Questions

1. Describe the culture of your church as you think it would appear to an outsider. Would others be able to identify a caring culture in your church?
2. Why is it important to use biblical categories to describe people's problems?
3. List some of the reasons Christians are called to care for one another in the church.
4. Why is it important that Jesus is the perfect example of a normal human being?

CHAPTER THREE

When the Church Doesn't Care

Let's go back to the story of Sam and Aisha. Sam texts Aisha to say he would like to see their son Jerome. Aisha replies that she doesn't trust Sam to care for Jerome because he is always drunk. She tells him to get help, and then he can spend time with Jerome. So Sam stops in at the church down the street on Sunday morning. After the worship service, he asks the pastor if they can talk. The pastor, John, tells him to call his office for an appointment. On Monday Sam calls and the church secretary mentions that Pastor John is pretty busy, but that he can come in the next week. When Sam finally talks with him about his marriage imploding and his problems with drinking, Pastor John gives him some numbers to call—an addictions counselor at the local mental health center, a marriage therapist, and a divorce lawyer (just in case). Sam leaves with a stack of papers, but no wiser on how to unravel his problems and without being offered biblical, Christ-centered hope for forgiveness, redemption, and change.

Perhaps your church would have a more caring approach to Sam's problems (I hope!), but would the end result be much the same? Is your church able to offer the soul care that Sam and his family need? And if not, why not?

It's surprising that even though Christ has given his church the responsibility to provide soul care and has provided us with everything necessary to do this good work, local churches so often do not provide soul care to their members and the surrounding community. I have noticed at least three overarching reasons why the church struggles with the task of soul care. The first is due to secular philosophies the church has embraced. The second, which is interwoven with the first, is that the church has abdicated many of its primary duties of discipleship and care for the broken in favor of techniques and methods born from worldly philosophies. Third, while we may know and believe the right things about God and his Word, obeying and applying them can be challenging. This chapter is an attempt to explain those reasons in a bit more detail. The goal is to spur church members and leaders to consider whether any of these elements are presently hindering their faithfulness in living out God's call to care for the souls of their community.

Last Resort

Sam actually reached out to a church for help, but for many the church is often the last resort for care. I can recall serving as an associate pastor as we fought against the tide to encourage our people to let us know of their needs and struggles. I say we fought against it, because the flow of the tide was for the church office to be the last place to know of particular needs within the body. Folks would say things like, "We know you're busy, and we didn't want to bother you." I was always deeply concerned to hear that they believed I was too busy to help them. In fact, I went out of my way to demonstrate that they were a first priority to me. As I have grown in the ministry, I have come to learn that they might have really been saying that they were too embarrassed to share their problems. For many others, they never considered the church as the primary place to get the kind of help they thought they needed. Folks would visit therapists and lawyers before they would think to come to us.

This dilemma is certainly evidence of a problem within the culture of the church. But before we place too much blame on the people, the church must ask, what has given them the impression that their problems are better dealt with elsewhere? To some degree people feel uncomfortable sharing their inner struggles with their pastor and perhaps even their Christian friends. It is as if there is a stigma associated with certain problems that are best talked about and addressed at places other than the church.

As leaders in the church, we need to address where such a stigma comes from and to take responsibility, where appropriate, for the ways have we contributed to the stigmatization of certain problems. What, if anything, can we do better in the future to erase these types of stigmas?

Diagnostic and Statistical Manual of Mental Disorders

In order to understand the context of the discussion regarding stigmas in mental health, we need to look a little more in depth at the *Diagnostic and Statistical Manual of Mental Disorders (DSM)*. As discussed in chapter two, the *DSM* is the primary reference text utilized by psychologists and psychiatrists to make psychological diagnoses. In 1970 when Jay Adams wrote his movement-shaping work *Competent to Counsel*, the *DSM* was only on its second edition, published in 1968. The *DSM* was not nearly as influential during those days. It was primarily used in psychiatric institutions as a common language to identify similar symptoms and guide consistent treatment with patients. All of that changed in the 1970s, with the work of Robert Spitzer.

Spitzer was the task force chairman for the *DSM*-III. He guided a dramatic shift in focus from a Freudian-based categorical system to one based upon biological psychiatry.

The watershed moment cannot be understated for its influence on counseling care and how the culture views human problems. Problems had been viewed as episodes of psychosis and neurosis, but now these same symptoms were placed within diagnoses assumed to have biological cause, or more specifically a neurological basis. That changed everything for the influence of psychiatry and more importantly the prolific and standardized use of the *DSM* in the mainstream of medicine, psychology, and culture. Once the *DSM* was viewed as an internal document intended to help practitioners, but now it has become the common cultural language utilized to categorize our internal human anguish and emotional turbulence.[1]

While biological psychiatry in the *DSM* is the dominant approach to mental health, there have been skeptics from the beginning. The diagnostic inflation resulting from the growth of the *DSM*'s influence, now on its fifth edition, has only increased the criticism of biological psychiatry. Interestingly, there has been a division among psychologists and psychiatrists regarding the "biological" approach. Psychologists attempt to highlight the similarity of outcomes for the depressed between the talk therapy they offer and the medical treatments offered by psychiatry. We are also seeing a growing number of psychiatrists raising concerns over the lack of scientific evidence to support the trajectory of psychiatry and its dominance in a flailing mental health system. Allen Frances, the *DSM-IV* task force chairman, said that the *DSM* diagnoses are only "fictive placeholders," or "useful constructs."[2] He continued to explain his concerns with the path psychiatry continues to move down: "The absence of biological tests is a huge disadvantage for psychiatry. It means that all of our diagnoses are now based on subjective judgments that are inherently fallible and prey to capricious change. It's like having to diagnose pneumonia without having any test for the viruses or bacteria that cause the various types of lung infection."[3]

My point is that the way we categorize emotional and behavioral distress must not be simplified to only biological causes. We are body and soul, so both must always be considered. This does not mean we do not have biological problems, but we cannot so easily disassociate the material from the immaterial as many of the *DSM* diagnoses suggest. Interestingly, the *DSM* itself never claims to know the etiology of the diagnoses listed in its pages. The introduction of the *DSM-5* states,

> The symptoms contained in the respective diagnostic criteria sets do not constitute comprehensive definitions of underlying disorders, which encompass cognitive, emotional, behavioral, and physiological processes that are far more complex than can be described in these brief summaries. Rather, they are intended to summarize characteristic syndromes of signs and symptoms that point to an underlying disorder with a characteristic developmental history, biological and environmental risk factors, neuropsychological and physiological correlates, and typical clinical course.[4]

The information described here is crucial to understanding the *DSM*. It does not provide insight into causality of the disorders. It uses brief summaries to systematically categorize common (and some uncommon) human experiences. The writers argue that the symptoms point to an underlying disorder, but the problem is that the underlying disorder is assumed by their philosophical approach, as mentioned in the previous chapter's discussion of the *DSM* and its lack of definition for "normal." Diagnoses have not been identified as disorders by scientific inquiry similar to the studies conducted by medical science. The writers further clarify the limits of the *DSM*'s diagnoses: "Nonclinical decision makers should also be cautioned that a diagnosis does not carry any necessary implications regarding etiology or causes of the individual's mental disorder or the individual's degree of control over behaviors that may be associated with the disorder."[5]

The *DSM* remains infused in our culture and is without any viable replacement. But there are discontents with the system, among elites in the disciplines of psychology and psychiatry.[6] Yet those attempting to integrate psychology with Christianity by and large seem to dismiss the critiques of "scientific rigor" in the *DSM* system. For now, the language of criteria and diagnosis in the *DSM* remains the prevailing norm in our culture.

Christians must consider at least a few concerns with the *DSM*. First, even those within the secular fields are criticizing the scientism which has created the prominence of the mental health language. Second, the reductionism of humanity to a simple biological entity is problematic because it is contrary to the biblical view that people are both body and soul. Third, the diagnoses dismiss the reality of sin and all of its effects on our humanity—both body and soul. For us as Christians it is a serious mistake to dismiss the noetic effects of sin (the effects of sin on the mind), the physiological decay of the body, and the biblical remedy provided for all the predicaments caused by the curse of the fall.

Creation of a Stigma

One major factor in the creation of a stigma associated with "mental health" is the *DSM*. We should all be grateful for any advancements in discovering organic causes of any abnormal symptoms, but we must not confuse organic disease with the labels of psychological disorders. The *DSM* does not claim to know the etiology, or cause, of any of the disorders. In fact, a mental disorder is defined as a syndrome, which is a collection of symptoms. The diagnostic labels described in the *DSM* are not in the same categories as organic diseases, although we have a powerful secular system that treats them as such.

A second contributing factor is that counseling became a specialized entity around the turn of the twentieth century when the pastorate became professionalized. The adoption of secular techniques and theories about humankind and their problems became prominent in the church. The pastor was no longer viewed as properly equipped to be the physician of the soul. The Word of God and prayer were viewed as too simplistic an approach for the complexities of new problems. Experts in the field of counseling psychology and the expanding influence of psychiatry set the language and agenda for categorizing human problems and various treatment plans.

Before long talk therapy became an essential part of our society. We were saturated with the language of the psychological explanations of people's problems and having a therapist became commonplace and viewed by some as an essential part of a flourishing life. In times past, the pastor played the role of the most wise advisor in matters of the soul. The day seems to have passed, but not without its consequences for the church.

Psychology still laments that social stigmas of mental disorders is one of their biggest problems. Many of the labels we use to classify human problems are now household language—people freely admit to labels they have been given, like depression, panic attacks, OCD, PTSD. I am grateful that our culture promotes more openness and transparency with our weaknesses. However, these labels are not viewed as simple descriptions but more as diseases with a biological basis that are resistant to any change. Even though the secular mental health system has spent lots of money on campaigns attempting to eliminate social suspicions, the labels carry with them a certain stigma.

There is not a secular system available that can explain the social ills of mental disorders without creating some form of stigma. While the Christian worldview provides context to understand our human weaknesses, biological or soulish, in a more normalized way, regrettably we still use the secular constructs. Actually, the Christian community has not discarded the stigmatization of mental health issues but exacerbated them. We must be honest about our failures here.

We have failed to care well for the broken. The fine line we walk is to maintain an uncompromising stance against sin, while displaying the wonderful riches of the grace of Christ to the broken sufferer and sin-wounded soul. I fully admit this is not a simple task and that we will, even with the best of intentions, make mistakes in our ministry discernment. However, we must be quick to repent and quick to make amends. We must err on the side of grace and kindness through hearts of compassion.

We have been guilty of admonishing when we should have been comforting and encouraging. But equally we have been guilty of excusing sin rather than having the courage to confront the destructive effects of sinful desires and behaviors. We have ostracized sinners and dismissed our own sins by promoting self-made righteousness. We have also been guilty of compromising biblical morality, welcoming open and unrepentant sinfulness in our midst. Both approaches are wrong and neither demonstrate the quality of care required of us in the Scripture. We are guilty, and may the Lord grant our collective repentance.

What were once described as moral musings or soulish vexations have now largely been recategorized as psychological disorders. The biblical category of sinner has been largely replaced with the secular categories of psychological diagnosis. The sinner can be redeemed and restored; the secular labels can only be coped with or managed. In order to remove the guilt and shame from a person who bears such a label, the secular culture made the symptoms a person experiences as a part of their identity. There is no true freedom from diagnostic labels. The hope behind the labels is that the guilt and shame of a person's experiences are removed. The system mimics a religious movement, offering care and relief from guilt and shame, all the while under a completely different paradigm.

The church has contributed to the stigmatization of mental health problems by accepting the secular narrative of the mental health system. The symptoms described are true human experiences and we should be forthright and clear to acknowledge them. But the system that explains the symptoms we experience is rooted in unbiblical ideas.

When we allow secular theorists to define problems of humanity in exclusively psychological terms rather than biblical terms, it becomes more difficult for us to see how the Bible speaks to those issues. The two most common examples of this are the common cultural understanding of disorders like anxiety or depression. Most of the population is convinced that our emotional or psychological problems are simplistically explained by some sort of biological malfunction. But, at this point, science has not definitively supported that narrative.[7]

The cumulative result, however, is that many of the problems common to humanity are seen as outside the scope of the Scripture. When we become convinced that the Bible does not address these human struggles and sorrows, the church disengages from the work of soul care because we are convinced the tools we have been given to proclaim and the culture we have been asked to cultivate are powerless to overcome some of our most significant problems or provide hope in the midst of our sorrows.

Thus, Christians must ensure that our starting point is not worldly systems or categories, but the truth of God as revealed in Scripture. And our understanding of sin and suffering must not be informed by just one passage, but by the *whole* counsel of God. If we fail to do so, we will err in our understanding of sin, suffering, and the very nature of humanity.

The practical result of this acceptance of secular categories to describe human problems is that Pastor John didn't feel equipped or even called to help Sam and his family. Since Sam's needs could be described in psychological terms, Pastor John believed that only a psychologist could help him. So he missed out on offering Sam the hope of change that comes with a heart turned to God and the power of repentance and faith to turn his life right side up through Jesus Christ.

This attitude contributes to the stigma of mental health because it teaches our members that no matter how much they desire to help someone who struggles, the problems the person is facing remains outside of their ability and the church's ability to help. We must contribute to changing the stigma of these problems, but it is not by accepting the psychological narrative. We must work to reclaim the sufficiency of Scripture for lasting hope in the most desperate of our human problems. The church is the institution to guard and defend this work in order to demonstrate the vitality of biblical community in loving the broken well.

What about Science?

One of the most common questions I receive from pastors objecting to the ideas of biblical counseling is regarding the "science of mental health." These pastors share my convictions regarding the sufficiency of Scripture and first order issues of doctrine. They believe in the power of the Holy Spirit and the vitality of the Word. They preach, trusting the Spirit to do his work through the Word. But something changes for them when they are one-on-one with a person suffering with deep emotional distress. There is a hindrance to trust the Word, because they believe they are dismissing the science which supports the mental health system.

Let me briefly address the issue of science. For far too long biblical counselors have been labeled as anti-science. From the beginning of the biblical counseling movement, Adams made clear that he was not against science, and we remain grateful for true scientific advances. "I do not wish to disregard science," Adams said, "but rather welcome it as a useful adjunct for the purposes of illustrating, filling in generalizations with specifics, and challenging wrong interpretations of Scripture, thereby forcing the student to restudy the Scriptures."[8]

I echo Adams's suggestion regarding science. I appreciate scientific advance and applaud uses born from them for the good of humanity. We must not confuse the common grace provided by medical discovery with our ultimate hope. However, we must be vigilant to discern the difference between science and scientism.[9] A vast chasm spans between the truth of science and what is speculated or theorized as science in the realm of psychology and psychiatry. Since that speculation serves the particular purposes in the secular world it comes under less scrutiny and often passes as common knowledge or even promoted as settled scientific knowledge.

Scientism, the use of scientific language to propagate philosophy or theory, seems to be reigning within the realms of psychology and psychiatry. There are many psychologists and psychiatrists recognizing the dangerous trajectory of the *DSM* system. They are lamenting the prominence of the system despite its lack of scientific evidence. Even before the newest release of the *DSM-5* in 2013 and especially since, psychiatrists and psychologists alike are lamenting the direction of the system and calling for distinct reform. The lack of scientific evidence behind key pillars of psychiatry, like the chemical-imbalance theory, are being revealed by research.[10] Yet, the church seems to be the last group to acknowledge the flaws of the secular system for fear of being labeled as non-progressive or anti-intellectual, even when leaders in the secular system are lamenting the lack of scientific rigor within their disciplines. My point is that we cannot and should not make assumptions about these secular philosophies—especially now that the secularists are questioning the scientific validity which has long been its fortification.

We would do well to heed the caution given by Francis Schaeffer years ago:

> I do not believe that man without absolutes, without the certainty that gave birth to modern science in the first place, will continue to maintain a high sense of objectivity. On one side, I think science will increasingly become only technology. On the other side, it will become sociological science and be a tool of manipulation in the hands of the manipulators. Beware, therefore, of the movement to give the scientific community the right to rule. They are not neutral in the old concept of scientific objectivity. Objectivity is a myth that will not hold simply because these men have no basis for it. Keep in mind that to these men morals are only a set of averages. Here, then, is a present form of manipulation which we can expect to get greater as one of the elites takes more power.[11]

The New Norm

In the early days of the biblical counseling movement, Jay Adams articulated the distinction between a biblical worldview and the secular humanism found in Sigmund Freud and Carl Rogers. But today psychiatry's medical model has also become a tour de force in a modern approach to care. As you study the mental health industry you will be hard-pressed to identify clearly defined norms, especially if you consider all the variations in talk therapy and psychiatry. Norms can be difficult to articulate, since there are such a variety of approaches to care in the secular world.

Eclecticism

One of my students recently asked an insightful question: "Dr. Johnson, you have taught us the three forces of psychology, but is there a fourth force?" The student was referring to the three predominant approaches identified when assessing the history of secular psychological theory: psychoanalytic theory proposed by Freud; then the behavior theory of Pavlov, Watson, and Skinner; and then the humanistic psychology of Maslow and Rogers. These broad forces were the schools of thought for much of the counseling psychology in talk therapy and were used as a basis to spurn new methodologies of care.

The context helps you to understand how I responded. At first, I explained that I was unaware of a true fourth school of thought that was distinguished in the same way as the first three. As I pondered the question further, I responded by saying that it seems *eclecticism* has become the fourth school of thought.[12] But we must be careful not to simply propose that biblical counseling is merely one more addition to the cacophony of eclectic theories that may be helpful to those struggling with soulish problems.

In the helping profession, there is a movement toward eclecticism. Talk therapists seem to approach care from a very inclusive perspective. At one time, counseling psychology was viewed in terms of unique systems of approach, like psychodynamic, Rogerian, behavioral, etc. What is in vogue at the moment is a smattering of methodologies used at the discretion of the therapist from an ever-expanding toolbox. Specific therapies which are viewed as working best for certain types of problems are employed from the toolbox, but other techniques may be added or subtracted depending on the flexibility of the therapist. Part of the issue here is that the supposed science utilized to support the use of various therapies, according to many, have less significant outcomes than once believed. Scientism—the use of scientific language to propagate a philosophical approach—is pervasive in both psychology and psychiatry—and it is rearing its ugly head in the form of eclecticism.[13] In many ways, adopting eclecticism is evidence that there is growing suspicion in "settled science" relating to biological psychiatry.

The approach makes sense with the broad acceptance of pragmatism in our secular culture over the last century. This "de-systematized" approach is consistent with the pluralism of our culture. The movement is not, however, limited to the secular world. Integrationists have followed the well-worn path of the secular therapists and have not wandered far. Eclecticism is prevalent for integrationists as well, as is clear from considering some of the more prominent figures from the movement.[14] The biblical counseling movement would do well to guard against the influence of this trend toward eclecticism, as we grow in solid biblical discernment and wisdom.

I should add that scientism has also become pervasive in the church offering a sophisticated covering for use of various secular philosophies. This approach makes sense from a secular worldview without absolute truths to guide wisdom, but a Christian worldview demands discernment and caution before we accept these cultural norms. We must avoid thinking of biblical counseling as merely one more addition to the cacophony of eclectic theories. We must caution against the movement toward eclecticism among biblical counselors by thinking that we need to add different types of methodologies and techniques from different systems which will expand our toolbox and make us more well-rounded counselors.

Cost of Cultural Relevance

Now that we have a small sense of how the ship was slowly turned, it is necessary to acknowledge the implications of adopting worldly approaches to care within the church. By the use of the term *worldly*, I do not mean devoid of legitimate care and concern, something inherently evil, or something we cannot acknowledge in human terms as good. What I am saying is that the type of care built upon the world's systems will only achieve the world's ends. This type of care can only obtain a shortsighted hope and help that is bound by the world and susceptible to its decay and destruction. As Carl Trueman says, "Cultural relevance can be a cruel mistress."[15] The desire to be intellectually relevant has tempted us to avoid dependence upon the Holy Spirit for supernatural power in favor of humanly devised wisdom.

What is at stake for the church if we continue to pursue the world's systems of care? There are many intricate and detailed ramifications that are worthy of consideration, but in this brief section let's consider several categories more broadly. These categories are representative of ways the church has been affected by the shift toward acceptance of modern pastoral care submerged in psychological theory. The deep and detrimental effect is that people are left destitute and without answers when the church abdicates her responsibility to stand for truth.

Our View of Sin and Suffering

I think we all agree that we need to be constantly growing in in our biblical understanding of human sin and suffering. Yet our "growth" in this discussion is often based more on secular concepts of human suffering than it is on biblical concepts. We must also remain cautious not to define human sin and suffering in *psychological* terms. The church has adopted many secular definitions like the *DSM* diagnostic categories, "recovery," "self-esteem," etc., which keep Christians from thinking biblically about human problems. Many believers view this as harmless or as advancements in our understanding of counseling and soul care. I believe the adoption of these secular definitions have hindered our ability as the church to minister well to those entangled in the consequences of sin or who are truly suffering the deep and dark effects of this cursed world. In the end, the church is hindered from truly engaging sinners and sufferers in a helpful way.

Another concern is that we are myopic in our views of sin and suffering from the Scripture and do not consider the whole counsel of God's Word as we formulate our understanding of care for sinners and sufferers alike. Often this comes in the form of holding on to a truth expressed in the Scripture without paying attention to other passages that counterbalance or nuance our understanding of that verse. For example, many well-meaning Christians inadvertently start sounding like Job's "comforters" when they try to discern a specific sin as the cause of a person's suffering. Does the Bible teach that sin brings suffering into our lives? Certainly! "Good sense wins favor, but the way of the treacherous is their ruin" (Proverbs 13:15). And yet, the Bible is also very clear that many of our sufferings cannot be traced back to a specific, personal sin. How many times has someone in the church blithely quoted Romans 8:28 to a suffering saint, saying that "all things work together for good," without first taking the time to obey the command in Romans 12:15 to "weep with those who weep"?

Our View of Humanity

In the church, we have also underestimated the impact of secular psychology's view of humanity. Any psychological theory or counseling method is a system of wisdom. Methods are not neutral in counseling care. Methodology is the practical outworking of what we believe to be true about the person, their problem, and the solution. So what you believe about the human condition will directly affect how you interpret someone's problems and how you guide those under your care. Psychological theories ushered in a very different view of humanity than that of biblical Christianity. An altered view of guilt and shame from Freud explains those human problems as originating from our past, instead of our failure to measure up to the standards of a holy God. Behavioral psychology promotes the reduction of our problems to biology only and gives rise to the idea that has permeated our culture that all mental health issues can/should be solved with medication. Or maybe we have adopted the idea that all we need to deal with struggles is positive thinking and believing that we have the power from within to build and strengthen the self. All of these ideas, based in secular thinking, are unbiblical views of humanity that offer superficial remedies to real human problems.

A biblical view of humanity contradicts these underlying secular assumptions. We shouldn't be surprised as Christians that our view of humanity is contrary to the world's. What is surprising, however, is the way the church has adopted the techniques, methodologies, and language of the world's system while thinking a biblical view of humanity would remain intact. Our view of humanity is not of secondary importance in counseling and care. We must remain consistent in our Christian view of men and women as both body and soul. We must remain consistent as we employ counseling techniques because they communicate our beliefs about people, their problems, and the solutions to those problems. For Christians, Jesus Christ must remain the centerpiece of our care for the broken because he is the centerpiece of God's care for the broken.

Much of the modern pastoral care movement, with good but misguided intentions, expanded unbiblical ideas of human nature to include a tripartite view that says people are partitioned into three separate domains: body, soul, and spirit. In this view, each of these domains have their own separate authority. The physician is for the body, the psychologist is for the soul, and the pastor is for the spirit. The main problem with this view, aside from the error of trying to neatly divide complex human beings into completely separate segments, is that it tends to divide us into unequal parts. The body currently dominates the discussion regarding human nature. Biological psychiatry has become the supreme paradigm accepted within our cultural context. But should Christians accept this paradigm?

At minimum, Christians should move with extreme caution and vigilance to reject the unbiblical ideas that are promoted. Modern thought has redefined the word "soul" to describe what could be observed in outward behavior. Therefore, psychology was redefined as the study of human behavior, experiences, and emotions.[16] This meant that the soul was no longer viewed as the inner person described as the seat of our emotions, affections, thinking, desires, and volition. No longer should God's Word have dominion over the inner person, but rather the modern *discoveries* of psychologists were made into *counseling systems* that have rule and authority.

The Bible, then, has been left to a very small spiritual portion of man. Many conservative Christian integrationists would say the Bible is authoritative and sufficient. They truly believe the Bible is sufficient for *spiritual problems*. But the issue lies with their limitation of the problems of humanity defined as "spiritual."

Most pastors are not alarmed by their thinking because they do not understand the limitations of the expressed *authority* and *sufficiency*. For conservative pastors those are necessary words which need to be expressed in order to gain a hearing. Yet, many pastors miss the implication of what is meant by the limitations of the words "authority" and "sufficient" found in integrative systems. It may be that some integrationists miss the implications as well. The description of human problems which exclude spiritual elements, unnecessarily limits our view of the sufficiency of Scripture to speak to problems the way our culture defines them.

Let me also be clear here. As mentioned earlier, I am not advocating a hyper-spiritual perspective that eliminates any physical element in our sins and sufferings. Rather, I am arguing that we must remember that a human is an embodied soul; we are both material and immaterial. We have problems of the soul, and we have physical ailments. However, while we have both, we must not assume that these two things are radically divided from one another. When we experience spiritual vexations in the form of temptations, anxieties, fears, jealousy, etc., the Bible tells us that these problems of the soul have an effect upon our bodies.

Proverbs 14:30 states, "A tranquil heart gives life to the flesh, but envy makes the bones rot." Not only do our internal struggles affect us physically, but an inner life of peace gives life to our bodies. Science has certainly indicated such a connection, although not in such spiritual terms. We are convinced that stress is bad for the body in a multiplicity of ways. Panic attacks, insomnia, overeating—these are just some of the physical manifestations of internal stress.

The state of our physical bodies also affects our spiritual well-being. A person who receives a diagnosis of cancer is not simply fighting a physical disease. They are fighting a physiological disease that also affects them spiritually. Cancer patients need to see their doctors and heed their counsel, but we must also consider the toll of such a diagnosis on a person's heart. They are face-to-face with their own mortality. As Christians, we know that death is a reality, but the diagnosis of a terminal illness can bring immediacy to that reality and cause intense wrestling in the soul. Cancer patients need someone to walk with them and help them put this physical suffering within the context of supernatural realities regarding sin, death, resurrection, and glorification. The glories of Christ Jesus are needed to anchor the soul from swaying with such a diagnosis. Of course, it must also be acknowledged that the diagnosis of a physical malady like cancer does not have a predetermined effect upon the soul. Many may respond with fear or anxiety. Others may respond with supernatural peace. But regardless of the response, our bodies and our souls are intertwined.

This is an important issue to grapple with because pastors and other members of the church can become paralyzed by fear in their desire to care well for hurting people. As long as the *DSM's* diagnoses are accepted without question, Christians are led to believe there is a clear scientific and biological cause for a person's struggles and are hesitant to offer help because they fear that they will hinder help coming from a different source. But, as will be unpacked further in the next section, the Word of God, rightly applied, is not a hindrance to true soul care. Instead, it is just what is needed to bring life that extends into eternity.

Our View of Scripture

The sufficiency of Scripture always has been and always will be critical to the discussion of soul care within the church. Every generation must preserve the Scripture's sufficiency, and our generation is no different. History has taught us, particularly during the Protestant Reformation, that dismissing the sufficiency of Scripture has consequences for our views on the authority of God's Word.

In our modern world, it can be easy to compromise the sufficiency of Scripture without overtly denying it. The secular diagnostic labels carry with them a worldview regarding potential causes and remedies, even though the labels are merely a collection of symptoms and not the scientifically validated diseases many believe them to be. When we utilize those labels, we often unknowingly circumvent our study of the Scripture to discover all that it has to say about those same human experiences. Dismissing Scripture or deferring to an alternate authority when the Scripture addresses those same symptoms is a practical proclamation that the Scriptures are insufficient to deal with the problems of our day. I would agree that the Scripture is insufficient to address the problems *as we have described them*. But the problem is not the insufficiency of Scripture, but the insufficiency of the labels we have given to our human struggles.

Since the natural man cannot discern the things of the spirit (1 Corinthians 2:14), most data regarding symptoms of human suffering are not categorized as having anything to do with the *spiritual* part of man. Therefore, it is surmised that other sources of authority, namely the social sciences, are necessary to address secularly created categories. In these cases, there is not a denial of the *sufficiency* or *authority* of Scripture because the problems are defined in clear terms outside of the scope or intention of God for giving his inspired revelation. So, the doctrines of sufficiency and authority may be upheld with a clear conscience. In reality, though, limitations are being imposed on the Scripture's definition of humanity and the domain of problems for which God has given sufficient revelation to address.

We ought to first be asking if the Scripture addresses these problems in any way and allow the Scripture its proper place of authority in giving us understanding by the illumination of the Spirit to assess and address these very real human problems. When we neglect the Scripture in this way, we not only dismiss the sufficiency of the Bible, but we compromise its authority and promote remedies to human problems that are temporary and fleeting.

Take for example the promotion of behavioral methods in many Christian parenting books. Many of those parenting techniques seem to accomplish the goals of conforming a child to outward obedience, but the heart of the child is often neglected. One time after preaching on a Sunday morning I went to the children's area to pick up one of my children. I noticed a Hot Wheels car in his hand. While we had many of those toy cars at home, this one did not look familiar. So I made him take the car back in to the teacher and confess what he had done. I remember being embarrassed that he was the preacher's kid and had taken something from the classroom.

The following week after my sermon, I noticed that he did not have anything in his hands when leaving the classroom.

I was happy that my son had learned not to take something that was not his, no matter how enticing. As we began to drive away, I looked in the review mirror as he pulled a Hot Wheels car out of his pocket. My quick-fix parenting, which focused on my son's behavior, did not address his heart. He did learn from my instruction—he learned to be a more sophisticated sinner! He had changed from the week before, but only externally. Rather than walk out of his class with the car in his hand, he put it in his pocket so that he would not be discovered. What didn't he learn? He didn't learn obedience to authority, a desire to honor authority, or to submit his desires to what God wanted for him. My quick fix hadn't addressed any of the real heart issues that were driving his behavior. This is just one small example of the many ways we can try to deal with human problems without addressing the heart by using God's Word. The effect is not simply a neutral result but a fueling of fleshly desires that produces more sophisticated and culturally acceptable sinning.

God's Word is sufficient to deal with the problems we face—including youngsters taking cars from Sunday school. Scripture does not always provide an immediate remedy, because a Christian worldview demands an eternal perspective. But we must not dismiss the eternal value of hope, peace, and restoration found in Christ as meaningless or insufficient.

The sufficiency of Scripture is demonstrated by the way in which we offer counsel. By *counsel*, I do not simply mean a formal or planned session of counseling but include, as David Powlison said, "Intentionally helpful conversations."[17] The things we say to one another when offering help in both formal and informal settings are examples of counseling. The wisdom to which we appeal in our counseling demonstrates our view on the sufficiency of Scripture regarding any particular subject. The Bible is about life, and God has "granted us all things that pertain to life and godliness" (2 Peter 1:3). He has "equipped [us] for every good work" (2 Timothy 3:17). And so, as we speak to one another in times of need, we must consider where our words are coming from because we always speak out of a commitment to some sort of wisdom or authority.[18]

Our View of the Church

Many reading this book will agree that our view of sin and suffering, our view of humanity, and our view of Scripture will consistently determine how we view and practice soul care. It seems to me, however, that there has been little discussion about how our understanding of the church affects our practice of soul care. I am certainly not the first to recognize detrimental changes to our concept of church,[19] but it is critical to highlight some of the contributing factors which have directly affected the church's ability to care well for the broken. While there are more contributing factors than the ones discussed in this section, the ones below seem most significant.

First, the modern American church's reluctance to practice church discipline has removed a critical method God intended to preserve the purity of his church and to care for his people. Church discipline was deeply affected by the church growth movement, and further detriment has been done by the therapeutic model of care influencing the church. At the same time, I do recognize the need for caution in this area; abuses of church discipline have certainly occurred in church history. Consider Gregory Wills's work in *Democratic Religion* where he recounts the ways churches were overbearing and legalistic in their use of church discipline. This overreach contributed to neglecting the practice altogether in favor of church growth principles as a replacement.[20] Legalistic or abusive expressions of church authority should be properly categorized as sinful and should not be tolerated. However, at the same time, the misuse of church discipline does not mean the church should abandon it altogether.

The second factor harming the church's practice of soul care is the specialization of pastoral ministry. When I considered a call to pastoral ministry, I never saw myself as a lead pastor who would preach every week. I believed that I was not very skilled in preaching, and was even a bit fearful of the task. I decided to pursue becoming an associate pastor who would teach and counsel. As I continued to grow and understand the Word of God with greater clarity, I realized that the call to pastoral ministry was a call to minister God's Word both privately in counseling and publicly in preaching. Pastoral ministry must not be reduced to only preaching *or* to only counseling. Neither the public nor the private ministry of the Word should be neglected.[21] However, many of our seminaries and churches currently overemphasize public ministry of the Word to the detriment of private ministry of the Word. Pastoral theologians once understood that pastoral work hinged upon the lived application of God's Word by dependence upon the power of the Holy Spirit. Now it seems that often, while we hold to sophisticated orthodox doctrinal statements, our pastoral care is disconnected from those roots. We have been guilty of underestimating the effects of sin on our emotional, physical, and mental well-being and thereby have minimized the usefulness of the Word of God by the power of the Spirit to make us at peace in the inner man.

Furthermore, the specialized approach to pastoral ministry follows the worldly, industrial patterns of prioritizing efficiency and expertise. I am not saying that it is wrong to have differing roles within church leadership nor that it is wrong to have some pastors who do more of the preaching while others do more of the counseling. My concern, however, is that we are excluding from our responsibility some pastoral duties that are clearly given to us in Scripture. Deferring clear pastoral duties to others who are more *specialized* or expertly trained in that area is an inexcusable dereliction of pastoral duties. The movement toward specialization in the church during the early part of the twentieth century has had lasting deleterious effects upon pastors and upon their care of God's people.

The third factor is closely related to specialization, because one of the results of specialization has been the professionalization of pastoral care. Seminaries began teaching clinical pastoral education in the 1930s and 1940s. Distinct departments began in clinical psychology and psychology of religion in order to distinguish the work of mental health counselor in churches from the soul work once done by the pastors. The change was intentional and had legitimate effects on how pastors viewed themselves and how churches viewed the role of the pastor. No longer was the pastor viewed as an expert trained in soul care, so church members began patronizing the trained professionals.[22]

The problem with this state of affairs is that Scripture places the responsibility for the care of souls on pastors. Pastors are to keep watch over the souls of their people, and they will have to give an account to the Lord for how they have fulfilled this responsibility (Hebrews 13:17). We are not free to simply create a professionalized model of soul care outside of the church when God places that duty square upon the shoulders of the elders of his church.

A significant consequence of the professionalization of soul care is that the "one another" commands regarding how we should engage in church fellowship have been overshadowed by professionalism. As believers we are called to encourage, edify, admonish, warn, teach, pray for, and love one another. We are to hold each other accountable so that we grow up into maturity in Christ (Ephesians 4:13–14; Colossians 1:28). Yet, the professional model of soul care has stripped the vitality of our Christian duty to one another. When problems occur, whether they are due to sin or suffering, our first inclination even within the church is to seek *professional* help. This pattern is a neglect of our biblical mandate to care well for one another.

The fourth factor is the approach to discipleship that is so prevalent among churches in America today. No longer is discipleship viewed as an intentional relationship that promotes the growth and sanctification of another individual by teaching them to obey all that Christ commands (Matthew 28:18–20). Now, discipleship is viewed as solely an intellectual education. Discipleship certainly is educational; Paul tells the Philippians, "What you have learned and received and heard and seen in me—practice these things, and the God of peace will be with you" (Philippians 4:9). But just because education is happening does not mean that discipleship is occurring. Modern educational theory operates on the assumption that as long as pupils are learning and their intellect expanding, they are growing. However, the simple passing along of information does not create a disciple. Discipleship is a whole-life pursuit, not simply an intellectual one. Discipleship incorporates both hearing and doing from a devoted heart.

Our View of God

In the twentieth century, the secular humanism and psychology that ushered in a therapeutic view of humanity also made a definitive statement about God. Everything we think, everything we say, and everything we do makes a statement about God. While a therapeutic view of humanity is devastating and hopeless for people with real hurt and real problems, the most detrimental aspect of our therapeutic views are its effects on how we see God.

Either God is erased from the humanistic worldview, or if we want to incorporate God within our worldview, he is simply a means to an end rather than the end itself. God becomes the means to our happiness and health. He is used as one source, among many, that may provide what is missing. When we take on this view of God, we seek him only for what he can do for us—to make us happy according to our own standards. What we "need" to thrive in this world is defined by a humanistic and therapeutic worldview.

When God does not meet our demands, he is viewed as harsh or unloving. While God is certainly the judge of all the earth and he will always do what is right, a therapeutic view leaves us in our guilt because God is viewed as an angry, unloving judge who we can never please. We become weighed down by our guilt and shame. We begin to believe that God does not welcome our contrition or shame, he only seeks to punish us. We see God not as someone who is inviting and forgiving, but as our enemy who could help us but refuses. We do not run to God as a first priority in our sin and suffering, but as a last resort. Yet, we know from Scripture this is not the character of our God as demonstrated in Christ, "Come to me, all who labor and are heavy laden, and I will give you rest. Take my yoke upon you, and learn of me, for I am gentle and lowly in heart, and you will find rest for your souls" (Matthew 11:28–29).

A therapeutic view of humanity also skews the way we understand the holiness of God. Our view of sin is jaded when we do not have a deep sense of the holiness of God. Either we will dismiss our sin and describe it in therapeutic terms, or we will be blinded to it because we do not see his perfection. A therapeutic view of humanity means we measure ourselves by other things instead of the holiness of God. Humility and brokenness can't grow in a heart that does not see the holiness of our God and our weak and frail disposition before him. We will not respond to God with contrition and gratitude, but entitlement and demand. In this way we do not see ourselves as broken and utterly dependent upon the lovingkindness and mercies of God, but more like Simon the magician, who simply wanted God as a means of power for self-improvement (Acts 8:9–24).

If we say that God does not address a human problem in his Word, we are communicating that God is aloof to our suffering. But consider how God has already demonstrated his care for humanity by being willing to suffer on earth as a human being, dying for us, and taking on himself the punishment that we justly deserve for our sins. Jesus, God in the flesh, demonstrated the posture of our trinitarian God toward those who suffer. He sought sinners, and he welcomed us who are weary and heavy laden. "Come to me," he said, "and I will give you rest." The pattern is that he takes our yoke of burden and gives us his yoke of righteousness and communion with God.

Consequences

There are several consequences that are inevitable when the church abdicates its primary duty to care for souls. First, sins are often recategorized in secular terms. For example, an addiction is not viewed as a problem of worship but as a biological weakness. Anger can be recategorized as intermittent explosive disorder. When we think like this, it is not soul care but the promotion of soul harm which encourages further entanglement in the strongholds of sin. It is harmful to individuals because in their struggles they do not see that their sin is keeping them from the deep and abiding hope in Christ.

Second, individuals will lack growth and maturity in Christ. So we are actually setting them up for further failure and making them vulnerable to the storms of life to be tossed to and fro (Ephesians 4:12–14). Without soul care being practiced and God's people being pointed to Christ, we are promoting a double-minded approach to life which does not make one at peace in life but unstable in all of their ways, according to James:

> If any of you lacks wisdom, let him ask God, who gives generously to all without reproach, and it will be given to him. But let him ask in faith, with no doubting, for the one who doubts is like a wave of the sea that is driven and tossed by the wind. For that person must not suppose that he will receive anything from the Lord; he is a double-minded man, unstable in all his ways. (James 1:5–8)

Third, not only are individuals affected by the church's abdication, but the church's witness is harmed as well. True fellowship among the body is lacking when deep caring for others is not a primary part of the culture of the church. We are not displaying the love for one another that Christ said marks us as his. The church that is not characterized by true sacrificial love for one another will be characterized by a culture that does not reflect the gentle and compassionate heart of Christ.

Conclusion

In the chapters that follow, I hope to demonstrate how God's design of the church, in both its essence and its functions, is intended to bear the responsibility of soul care. While different types of care are available in our secular culture, as Christians we must offer care consistent with the absolute truths granted to us from Scripture. The care we offer must seek to truly understand human hurt and at the same time care for the hurting in God's way. We will consider our submission to Christ, his care for us as our great Shepherd, the public and private ministry of Christ's under-shepherds, and the equipping of the saints for the care of souls. God has called the church to be a culture of care, and he has granted us his Word and the Holy Spirit for this difficult but worthy task.

Discussion Questions

1. Look again at the reasons mentioned for why a church might not practice soul care. Do any fit your church? If so, which ones?
2. How does the *DSM* contribute to the stigma of mental health problems?
3. How has the church contributed to the stigma of mental health problems?
4. How does a secular view of human problems affect the church's approach to soul care?
5. How does a therapeutic view of humanity affect our view of God?

CHAPTER FOUR

Christ as the Head
of the Church

Perhaps by this point in the book you are beginning to see the
need for your church's culture to change—to become a community that is maturing and learning to care for all with the
love of God. But how can that happen? If you know anything
about culture and church, you know that neither is easily
changed. The good news is that because we are Christians,
there is always hope for change. The change that is needed
can only be accomplished by the head of the church—Jesus
Christ. As head of the church, Jesus provides both the pattern
and the power for the church to provide soul care.

The functions of the church—the things we do together as
a body of Christ—must flow from the essence of the church.
Who we are will always determine what we do. So before
we discuss how the church can serve God's purpose to care
for his people, we need to focus on two essential truths—the
centrality of Christ as the head of the church and the vital
importance of our submission to him. These truths must be
understood and lived out if we are to grow in Christlike care
in his church. As Jim Elliot said, it is to Christ that we must
look for the pattern of how to glorify God in our life together.

The pivot point hangs on whether or not God has
revealed a universal pattern for the church in the New

Testament. If He has not, then anything will do so long as it works. But I am convinced that nothing so dear to the heart of Christ as His Bride should be left without explicit instructions as to her corporate conduct. I am further convinced that the 20th century has in no way stimulated this pattern in its "churching" a community, so that almost nothing is really "working" to the glory and pleasure of God. Further, it matters not at all to me what men have done with the church over there or in America, it is incumbent upon me, if God has a pattern for the church, to find and establish that pattern, at all costs.[1]

Elliot rightly recognized the pragmatism that has pervaded the church for far too long. Much of our approach has been to maintain a semblance of confessional adherence while preferring practices originating from the world rather than from the sufficient Scripture. The points that follow are an attempt to reclaim the supremacy of Christ as the one who leads and guides his church, and the one we must submit to in everything we do. Submitting to Jesus's plan for his church as found in Scripture will then guide our practices of soul care within the church.

The Authority of Christ

The first critical doctrine is that Jesus Christ is head of his church. Paul, by the inspiration of the Spirit, proclaimed that God "put all things under his [Jesus] feet and gave him as head over all things to the church, which is his body, the fullness of him who fills all in all" (Ephesians 1:22–23). The Puritan John Owen affirmed this truth by saying, "Christ's glory is seen in the fact that he alone was fit and able to be the head of this new family."[2] Lambert likewise rightly asserts, "Jesus is at the center of effective biblical counseling because he occupies the center of Christian theology. He is at the center of Christian theology because he is at the center of all of life."[3] To take his thought a step further, since Jesus is at the center of Christian theology, he is at the center of ecclesiology, our understanding of the church. In this chapter we will consider the way in which Christ, as head of the church, establishes the ministry of the church as a ministry of soul care.

In our day, the concept of headship tends to be resisted as an inherently evil hierarchical power structure. Thus, for modern ears, it may sound odd to proclaim that Christ is the head of his church. Abuses by politicians, pastors, husbands, and many others have created an almost involuntary response of distaste for authority.

We can and should stand against any abuses of authority, whether in governments, churches, or homes. At the same time, we cannot abandon the God-ordained idea of authority altogether. There are two basic errors, or sinful patterns, that consistently occur with the issue of authority. First, the error of tyranny or lording over someone is sinful abuse. Second, it is sinful when proper authorities are passive. If an authority does not fulfill their God-given role, it is harmful to those under their care (Jeremiah 6:12–18; Ezekiel 34:1–6).

Jesus is our head, which means he possess all authority. For many who have endured abuse at the hands of those who held power or authority, that may be difficult to hear. My desire, however, is that God's people do not dismiss legitimate, godly, good authority. Even if our rebellion against God's authority is not overt, a dismissal or ignoring of the authority that is given by God is also a form of rebellion.

The Scripture says that Christ is our head and that we are his body (Colossians 1:18). He gave himself for us. He stood in our place. Those who repent and believe are his beloved—we have been grafted into him. Certainly, this is not on the basis of our own merits but by grace through faith alone (Ephesians 2:8–9). We are his great reward. We, a bunch of ragtags, have graciously found favor with God through our great Head, the Lord Jesus Christ. Owen tenderly affirms, "So Christ says of his church, 'This is now bone of my bones, and flesh of my flesh. I see myself, my own nature in them, so to me they are beautiful and desirable.'"[4]

The headship of our Lord is to be celebrated as it is our duty and delight to live under his lordship! His tenderness toward us is proven by the fact that even while we were still sinners, and completely unlovable, he died for us (Romans 5:8). Christ has been appointed as head of the church rather than any earthly authority. My primary point is not only to reaffirm this doctrine, but also to illuminate how church practice should flow from this truth.

Paul declares clearly that "Christ is the head of the church, his body" (Ephesians 5:23). Leaving no doubt, the apostle said the reason is "that in everything he [Jesus] might be preeminent" (Colossians 1:18). Christ rules and reigns over all. We are not simply told that Jesus created all things, but we are also told that all things were created for him. All things are held together by him. What exactly are we to make of this declaration, and what does it really mean for us as a gathered assembly of believers? What practices are implied by the doctrine of Christ's headship?

Subtle Dismissal

Intellectually, no Christian would argue with the rightful position Jesus occupies as head of the church. Our primary duty as believers in the assembly of the church is to exalt Christ and to demonstrate our love and adoration for him by our obedience to him as our head.

However, we have forgotten Christ as our head in how we practice soul care. The sad reality is that much of our pastoral care for the last eighty years has relied on psychology and psychiatry, which have decidedly different philosophical presuppositions. Psychology offers an unbiblical view of hamartiology—they believe that humanity's basic problem is *not* that our sins have separated us from God. Since sin is not our basic problem, psychology can then offer a soteriology—a means of hope, change, and salvation—apart from a biblical Christology. When you add both of those together, we do not get a companion to aid our care to broken humanity, but a competing philosophy that is not according to Christ. We have been held "captive by philosophy and empty deceit, according to human tradition, according to the elemental spirits of the world, and not according to Christ" (Colossians 2:8).

Humans are certainly skilled at conjuring up empty philosophies. American self-reliance, self-esteem, health and wealth are just a few of the many frameworks that have shaped our earthbound practices of soul care. Ed Welch identified this danger when he said, "If sin is not our primary problem, then the gospel of Jesus is no longer the most important event in all of human history."[5] The result, when we choose to run after competing means of hope and change, is that our gospel care recedes from resting under the capable headship and secure promises of Christ.

Our modern Christian care models have divorced themselves from clear and sound doctrine in favor of humanistic philosophy. They present unbiblical views of our human problems, and, therefore, offer unbiblical solutions. The "Christian" use of these theories of self-sufficiency have only further confused and deceived us into thinking we have some power within to overcome our deepest problems. Yet, the Scripture is clear that we are to "put no confidence in the flesh" (Philippians 3:3). Rather, in Christ are hidden all the treasures of wisdom and knowledge, so the church must follow him and find our sustenance in him. He is the source of life—not simply life in being saved from death through justification, but the abundant life that results in walking by faith, with the Spirit as our helper and guide. The result is growth in sanctification.

Paul did not hesitate to correct professing believers who were being swept away by empty philosophy. We too need this constant reminder. For it is not as if all of these alternative descriptions of people and their problems do not offer tinges of reality. As Powlison states, "error must borrow elements of truth to be plausible."[6] This is why and how we are regularly deceived. We must be corrected by Scripture and submit to the authority of Christ as our Head. Paul had to remind the believers in Colossae of the preeminence of Christ and that Christ is their Head, to correct their drift toward vain deceptions.

But never forget that Jesus enacts his headship as a shepherd. We may not expect authority to be kind, gentle, or loving. But Jesus demonstrates proper headship with his gentleness and care for his sheep.[7] He does not compromise his commands because he knows they bring life and restoration to us. At the same time, he deals gently with us in our broken estate.

The Church's Submission to the Authority of Christ

How should we respond, as the body of Christ, to his loving headship? We must express our love to him by submitting to his authority. "If you love me," Jesus said, "keep my commandments" (John 14:15). As our head, Jesus uses us, his body, to accomplish his work. But that work is done according to his Word and by the power of the Spirit that he gifted to us. Ultimately it is Christ who works in us and through us (Philippians 2:13).

Jesus said he would do it—he promised to build his church (Matthew 16:18). Remember the discussion between our Lord and Simon? Jesus began with that most pivotal question, "Who do you say that I am?" Peter replied, "'You are the Christ, the Son of the living God.' And Jesus answered him, 'Blessed are you, Simon Bar-Jonah! For flesh and blood has not revealed this to you, but my Father who is in heaven. And I tell you, you are Peter, and on this rock I will build my church, and the gates of hell shall not prevail against it'" (Matthew 16:15–18).

The book of Acts teaches us that what Jesus promised to build he willingly fulfills. To this day he is still building his church. We must not confine the building of his church to the simple addition of people. We must also consider the spiritual growth in building a people firm and complete upon the great confession of Jesus as "the Christ, Son of the living God."

Thanks be to God that he saves us not simply to provide a light in our own hearts, but to shine a light into the darkness of the world around us. Jesus is building his church right here in the middle of our messy lives. He does this through the functions he has commanded the church to perform. As he matures us and conforms us to his image, he is building his church. We are not permitted to build the church in any way we please.

The Functions of the Church

One way in which our modern church culture has failed has been by adopting pragmatism as a primary lens through which we make decisions. Our appetite for pragmatics has decreased our patience with the slow process of change in people and has reduced our conscious dependence upon God for help and hope. Pragmatism rears its ugly head in a variety of ways—sometimes we can see it in trying to entertain instead of disciple the men, women, and children under our care; and at other times we can see it in our desire to not speak against sin or in not wanting to do the hard work of caring for the suffering. The functions of the church must always flow out of God's eternal truth. Each of the functions of the church serves our personal discipleship and provides opportunities for each of the members of the body to participate in the discipleship of others.

The functions mentioned below are not an exhaustive or comprehensive explanation. Each of these components of the church have received full-length book treatments. My goal in this section is to spur your mind to think of the beauty of these functions as more than rituals, as more than programs. The functions are intended to be means of soul care under the jurisdiction of the church.

Evangelism

Evangelism is soul care. The rescue of a person from the domain of darkness to the marvelous light has massive implications for the stability of the human soul. Paul tells us in Romans 5:1 that because of our faith in Jesus we are now at peace with God. Believers can now see more clearly—their eyes are opened to their own sins, but also to Jesus who has covered their sins with his righteousness. When a sinner repents, the angels rejoice—but it does not mean their problems are all removed. They can now see things that the natural person, with unsaved eyes, cannot see (1 Corinthians 2:14). Not only are we at peace with God, but we are free to live for Christ rather than being bound to live for ourselves (2 Corinthians 5:14). The person who has been saved is now secure in Christ and no longer needs to fear death because Christ has overcome it. All of this happens by faith, and faith comes by hearing the Word. Our first experience of soul care is the power of the Spirit regenerating our hearts by faith, which then enables us to believe in the Word of God.

Believers are called ministers of reconciliation to carry the message of the gospel in "jars of clay" (2 Corinthians 4:7). Sharing the good news of Christ is one primary way the church is commissioned to care for souls. Evangelism is one way that we imitate Christ by learning to lay down our own life—putting aside our fears and concern of reputation—for the sake of others, so that they may have their heart of stone be turned into a heart of flesh. Evangelism is deep soul care that engages in spiritual warfare for the good of another so that they may have life abundant and eternal.

Discipleship

The great commission of our Lord calls us to "make disciples." We are not charged simply with the winning of souls, but the growing of souls to stable abiding in the Lord Jesus. We should not miss that God's plan for the church in making disciples is to grow people to maturity by teaching them "to observe all that I have commanded." This ministry of teaching and growing to maturity is caring for souls.

In Colossians 2, Paul tells us that in the same way in which you receive the Lord Jesus, so walk in him. At least in part, our walk with Christ entails the Spirit convicting our hearts of sin so that we may repent and be strengthened to live by faith. Dr. Martin Lloyd Jones says it this way: "We have not merely been saved that we might escape hell; we have been saved in order that God may present a people which will astonish the whole world."[8]

Jesus gave the means not only for justification but also for sanctification, so that we can align our lives more and more with the reality that Christ is Lord. Our submission to Christ's authority is demonstrated by our growing obedience to all that he commands as we walk by the Spirit. Discipleship is what we call the process of helping another walk with Christ and be conformed to his image.

Many of our current approaches to discipleship dehumanize the process, as if discipleship were some sort of mechanized process whereby we automatically grow. Growth, however, does not occur without the engagement of all of our human faculties, including the wrestling of our emotions, the bending of our will, the changing of our behaviors, and more. Discipleship is organic; it cannot be programmed because it involves the application of God's eternal truths to the everyday moments and experiences of our lives. It is a conforming of our whole lives to the pattern of normalcy shown to us in Christ.

Discipleship does not happen simply through a one-hour-per-week Bible lesson. Discipleship happens through teaching and admonishing. The teaching that happens in our church Bible classes is an important component, but it is not enough. Teaching must be connected to help from others. We are taught, and then as we strive, with all of our human faculties, to live faithfully to the teaching of Scripture, we need others intimately involved in our lives who can offer correction and encouragement to help us live what we have been taught. I usually do not hear a truth and then immediately live it out. I need people in my life who can admonish, remind, and encourage me to be faithful as I grow to maturity in the Lord. We need to live life in close proximity to others who are also wanting to honor Christ as Lord. Sometimes we learn best by being a witness to how others live faithfully under the Lordship of Christ.

One example of this in my own life was a frequent, and often impromptu, meeting of several young married couples and their children after Sunday evening service at the house of an older couple in the church. The gatherings were always informal, but never meaningless or unintentional. Strong relationships were forged so that when the young married couples experienced trouble, the first place they would go for help is to that couple's house. It was a place of love, comfort, and support, even when difficult truths needed to be shared. I was one of the children who went along with one of the couples week after week, year after year. Witnessing these types of relationships made a deep impression on me as a depiction of the beautiful fellowship of the body. I rarely participated in discussion and was most often nestled in a corner of the room, but I observed, as a young child and later as a teenager, a deep love and devotion to one another that flowed out of an authentic faith in Jesus. This is the work of soul care entrusted to the church.

Counseling ministry is simply the overflow of the normal discipleship process of the church. As an individual encounters an intense problem in their life, intensive and focused discipleship becomes necessary. Devoted one-on-one, formal meetings are necessary for addressing an acute problem. The purpose of biblical counseling is to help individuals grow in maturity and sanctification as they learn to address their sin and suffering in a way that glorifies the Lord and is for their good. Thus, Jesus not only builds his church by adding to the number of those being saved; he also builds the church by adding to the depth and maturity of those he has saved.

Ordinances

Baptism and the Lord's Supper are two vital practices of the church. We must be careful to not dismiss their value for the care of the church. First, baptism is an act of obedience whereby an individual publicly proclaims faith in Christ and identifies with the fellowship of believers. This public proclamation is the ground upon which a member enters into the intimate care and responsibility of the church. The act of baptism itself is not salvific, but it does proclaim the death, burial, and resurrection of our Lord as well as the cleansing from sin granted by his substitutionary work. Baptism acts as a stake in the ground for believers to be held accountable and cared for by the body of Christ.

The Lord's Supper is a vital part of church fellowship whereby we remember the work of Jesus for the forgiveness of our sins—we "proclaim the Lord's death until he comes" (1 Corinthians 11:26). Communion is a means of care for our souls in part because it provides us with a regular opportunity to examine ourselves before the Lord. Proper examination of our inner man always means seeing ourselves in the mirror of God's Word. That alone can be dangerous because the Word reveals the depth of our wickedness. The fellowship meal binds the self-examination of our hearts with the vital remembrance of the sacrificial death of Christ and his triumph over sin. Although our wickedness is deep, our guilt and shame have been removed by the work of Christ. We need to be reminded of this truth often. The meal demonstrates that true biblical care reveals the depths of our hearts, but never without the balm of Jesus's work to cover our wounds. It is in his work we find comfort and solace.

Church Discipline

Life in Christ begins with the idea that we are needy people. When we see ourselves as needy, we will also appreciate the method of care that God has provided in church discipline. The goal of church discipline is to produce righteousness and restoration in the lives of believers. We should not think of church discipline primarily in terms of excommunication. Putting someone out of the church sometimes must happen in a biblically faithful church, but that is not the church's goal or the first step it takes in enacting church discipline. Church discipline begins with one-another relationships. Brotherly entreaty, caution, and warning are key when thinking about church discipline as a means of soul care.

"Discipline," Adams says, "is inextricably linked to education."[9] The Lord uses his church as one intentional means to discipline us so that we may grow in maturity. The Father disciplines the one he loves, so we must see God's love through discipline in the church. God's love for us cannot tolerate persistent, unrepentant sin because sin damages and leads to destruction.

We often think of the first step in church discipline as talking to the offending brother one-on-one. But Jesus taught that an essential first part of that first step is self-examination. Matthew 7:3–5 tells us to take the log out of our own eye before we take the speck out of our brother's eye. This self-examination does not dismiss an offense, but it does help us to see an offense through a clearer lens. When we examine ourselves before God, we are more likely to approach our brother with humility, gentleness, and the desire to restore rather than the desire to accuse and respond out of any defensiveness or bitterness caused by the offense.

Going to each other one-on-one to lovingly address sin should be a common occurrence since we are called to live as a family of God in close proximity with one another, and we are all still wrestling with indwelling sin. This type of discipline happens in my house every day. With eight sinners living in close proximity to one another, we tend to offend each other more than I would like to admit. But the goal is to maintain short accounts by dealing with the offenses in short order. Quickly addressing offenses is good for both parties involved. No one in the church is above this discipline, and the truth is that we all need it from time to time.

This daily care is a part of the lifeblood of the church. Church discipline should encourage us not to simply be hearers of the Word, but doers "until we all attain to the unity of the faith and of the knowledge of the Son of God, to mature manhood, to the measure of the stature of the fullness of Christ, so that we may no longer be children, tossed to and fro by the waves and carried about by every wind of doctrine, by human cunning, by craftiness in deceitful schemes" (Ephesians 4:13–14).

In the case that the brother or sister does not repent, we are to go to him or her with two or three witnesses. Again, the whole purpose behind Matthew 18 is that we forgive like Christ and desire to see the lives of our brothers and sisters in Christ displaying the righteousness of God. We are seeking restoration so that they repent and walk rightly with God. If we did not care about others, we would let them continue to be destroyed by the sin, which harms them and those around them. If we do not care well for the brothers and sisters in our community, it shows we are not zealous for the character of Christ to be formed in them.

On the rare occasion when a brother or sister still does not repent, then we are to tell it to the church. The goal is to make the church aware in order to plead with them and pray for them so that they can be restored to fellowship. The whole process is for the purpose of restoration. We want to see our brothers and sisters walking faithfully in fellowship with God and others. Sadly, if they do not repent, we are called to put them out of church fellowship—no longer invited to participate in the fellowship meal because the remembrance of forgiveness in the Lord's death on the cross is not theirs to celebrate. The church should not give them a false sense of peace when they are not living at peace with God.

Effective church discipline leads to growth in the body. The growth produced by church discipline may not be wider, but it is deeper. What do we hope for in a church that is growing? Are we only seeking numerical growth? Growing in numbers is great, but we would agree it is not always a healthy measurement of true growth. An equally important measure of growth is to see members of the body grow in maturity. Church discipline, as a means of care faithfully practiced in accordance with the Word, facilitates that spiritual maturity.

One primary hindrance to church discipline, however, is when we do not take the time to be known or to know others in the body of Christ well. It is difficult to offer corrective care when you know very little about someone. Even more difficult is being able to respond to corrective care when you do not know the other person well. Corrective care is easier to hear when we know the other person loves Christ deeply, loves us, and is willing to speak the truth because he has our best interest in mind.

As I discussed in chapter three, "When the Church Doesn't Care," there have been abuses of church discipline. Yet, we should not respond to sinful abuses of biblical practices by dismissing them altogether. Rather, we should make it our goal to practice church discipline appropriately in obedience to God, for the good of the church, and the restoration of the individual. Church discipline, when practiced biblically, is another primary means of soul care provided by God as the responsibility of the church.

There is a healthy tension for us in the church in learning how to remain dependent upon the work and power of Christ while at the same time fulfilling our responsibilities to serve God's people (Philippians 2:20). The fact that Jesus will build his church is not an excuse for us to do nothing. Instead, Jesus's headship should energize us to do his work while recognizing that Christ is working in us and through us. It is a reminder that we should not boast in our giftings or strengths. We do not have anything we did not receive (1 Corinthians 4:7). God is the Father of lights, from whom comes all good things (James 1:17). He will build his church! We exalt the headship of Christ as we honor his position and obey his ways of building up his church. As we do so, we display to the world his matchless grace.

For the Glory of Christ

Another implication of the headship of Christ is that our *primary* goal in soul care should not be to make someone feel better—it should be to glorify Christ. And when we glorify Christ in how we counsel one another, we will also be of most help to each other. If the glory of Christ is the stated goal of our life, then it makes sense that God has provided the means for us to accomplish that work through his word.

The functions of the church must be carried out by the Word of God and the power of the Holy Spirit. The Bible says that the Spirit testifies of Christ. The Holy Spirit's primary aim in the world is to point to the power and glory of Christ, in much the same way that the life and work of Christ pointed to the glory of the Father. If life is *all* about the glory of God, then the soul care in our churches should not aim short of that goal. This means we use the Word, the sword of the Spirit, to accomplish his work in the lives of the individuals who make up our local church body. As the Spirit works in the ordinary details of our lives, the Spirit testifies of Christ. Why? Because the aim of our lives is to bring glory to Christ, even in our suffering.

Luther's hymn, "A Mighty Fortress Is Our God," rings true as we strive to be faithful to that reformation truth that the Scripture is sufficient for both faith and practice.

Did we in our own strength confide, our striving
would be losing,
were not the right Man on our side, the Man of
God's own choosing.
You ask who that may be? Christ Jesus, it is he;
Lord Sabaoth his name, from age to age the same;
and he must win the battle.

Conclusion

There are times, based on our human perception, when it
seems as though Christ has forgotten his promise to build
his church. The things we see happening around us, the turmoil we feel inside, the desperate situations we are aware
of globally, those moments when it seems as though evil is
winning and chaos is abounding—at those times, Christ's
promise to build his church can seem empty. These are the
moments when our problems seem to block out our memory
of the truth and cloud our sight of the promises. When we
lose sight of the promises of God, we fail to see value and
hope in the means he provides to fulfill his promises.

Surely, we think, there is an easier way. We must all confess we enjoy the path of least resistance. We default to the
wide and narrow, the more efficient, the better way. After all,
we are taught to work smarter and not harder. That saying
makes sense when it is our strength that is on the line, but it
is not the best advice when working in God's economy.

All the means of Christ to accomplish his work are
not based upon expedient pragmatics, but upon nonnegotiable and unchanging truths. The confession of Christ as
the Son of God is the unalterable position from which he
builds his church. It is not simply a label we have given to
him, but a firm confession of truth, regardless of our actions

or attitudes. The way in which Jesus builds his church is fleshed out from this unchanging, confessional truth.

Discussion Questions

1. If we want our churches to grow in having a culture of care, why must we start with the headship of Christ and submitting to him?
2. What functions of the church are means of soul care?
3. How has the Spirit used these functions to care for your soul? Give one or two examples.
4. What are some of the reasons we might not trust in Christ's power to build and use his church?

CHAPTER FIVE

Christ as Our Good Shepherd

When we hear Jesus described as the shepherd of his people, we aren't meant to think of a Hallmark card picture of Jesus with flowing hair surrounded by little lambs. Instead, we are to see Jesus's role as shepherd as the God-intended complement to his strength and leadership. Jesus as shepherd provides the perfect disposition for his position as head of the church.

The rule and authority of Jesus is always tethered to love and gentleness. For us who believe he is our Lord and Chief Shepherd. Jesus is not *either* head *or* shepherd, but *both* head *and* shepherd. That means we are to obey his commands and to believe that he cares deeply for us in both obedience and disobedience. Jesus is invested in us. He has given himself for us. It is in the love of our Savior displayed in his shepherding that helps us trust his headship. That care is seen most clearly at the cross—it is his suffering as the Lamb of God that helps us trust him as Lord.

Jesus the Great, Good Shepherd

Jesus was revealed as our great shepherd in the Old Testament. Psalm 23 may be the most famous expression of our Lord as shepherd, but it is certainly not the only place we see that description. Jeremiah 6 and 8 reveal the inadequacies and dangers of human shepherds. When shepherds are not leading well, there is an effect on the flock. Ezekiel 34 is similar to the passages in Jeremiah, indicting the shepherds of Israel because they were not leading the sheep well.

> The word of the LORD came to me: "Son of man, prophesy against the shepherds of Israel; prophesy, and say to them, even to the shepherds, Thus says the Lord God: Ah, shepherds of Israel who have been feeding yourselves! Should not shepherds feed the sheep? You eat the fat, you clothe yourselves with the wool, you slaughter the fat ones, but you do not feed the sheep. The weak you have not strengthened, the sick you have not healed, the injured you have not bound up, the strayed you have not brought back, the lost you have not sought, and with force and harshness you have ruled them. So they were scattered, because there was no shepherd, and they became food for all the wild beasts. My sheep were scattered; they wandered over all the mountains and on every high hill. My sheep were scattered over all the face of the earth, with none to search or seek for them." (Ezekiel 34:1–6)

Both the passage in Jeremiah 6 and the one above in Ezekiel 34 describe the deleterious effects of poor shepherding upon the flock. After the indictment of the shepherds of Israel, the prophet Ezekiel shares a word from God promising that he will provide a shepherd to care for his people.

> For thus says the Lord GOD: Behold, I, I myself will search for my sheep and will seek them out. As a shepherd seeks out his flock when he is among his

sheep that have been scattered, so will I seek out my sheep, and I will rescue them from all places where they have been scattered on a day of clouds and thick darkness. And I will bring them out from the peoples and gather them from the countries, and will bring them into their own land. And I will feed them on the mountains of Israel, by the ravines, and in all the inhabited places of the country. I will feed them with good pasture, and on the mountain heights of Israel shall be their grazing land. There they shall lie down in good grazing land, and on rich pasture they shall feed on the mountains of Israel. I myself will be the shepherd of my sheep, and I myself will make them lie down, declares the Lord GOD. I will seek the lost, and I will bring back the strayed, and I will bind up the injured, and I will strengthen the weak, and the fat and the strong I will destroy. I will feed them in justice. (Ezekiel 34:11–16)

Martin Bucer highlighted the language of shepherding in his classic work *Concerning the True Care of Souls,* written during the Reformation. Arguably the most significant book on the topic of pastoral shepherding for nearly half a millennium, Bucer presented an exposition of Ezekiel 34 to outline his view of pastoral shepherding modeled after the work of Jesus, our chief shepherd. While the shepherding metaphor does not encompass all of the work of Christ, it certainly captures the application of primary tenets of his work. Bucer highlights the truths from Ezekiel that point to the work of Jesus as our shepherd: Jesus seeks the lost, brings back the strayed, binds the broken, and strengthens the weak as he feeds and protects the sheep.

Thomas Oden calls shepherding the "pivotal analogy" in the description of Christ and the work of pastors as his under-shepherds.[1] We see the fulfillment of Old Testament passages in Jesus's declaration in John 10 where he identifies himself as the shepherd of the sheep. He has come to lay down his life, protect us from the thief, and give us life—abundantly.

> So Jesus again said to them, "Truly, truly, I say to you, I am the door of the sheep. All who came before me are thieves and robbers, but the sheep did not listen to them. I am the door. If anyone enters by me, he will be saved and will go in and out and find pasture. The thief comes only to steal and kill and destroy. I came that they may have life and have it abundantly. I am the good shepherd. The good shepherd lays down his life for the sheep." (John 10:7–11)

> Jesus is the great Shepherd because of his work as the Lamb. He lays down his life for us so that we may do what is pleasing and live at peace. (Matthew 11:28–30)

> Now may the God of peace who brought again from the dead our Lord Jesus, the great shepherd of the sheep, by the blood of the eternal covenant, equip you with everything good that you may do his will, working in us that which is pleasing in his sight, through Jesus Christ, to whom be glory forever and ever. (Hebrews 13:20–21)

It's so important to remember that we are sheep—and that sheep need a shepherd. Our hearts will be shepherded by something or someone. I fear that for many the doing of

God's will has been replaced by the seeking of our happiness and peace by our own means. Secular culture becomes our shepherd rather than the Good Shepherd. But life abundant can only be found in him and through him.

The Shepherd Cares for His Church

The title of "sheep" might seem insulting to some, but it is certainly an accurate description for us. We are full of fears and insecurities. All people are sheep, and all people have wounds, but not all sheep have a shepherd to bind their wounds.

One way the Bible distinguishes between believers and unbelievers is by the using the categories of sheep and goats. But there are other passages where unbelievers are referred to as sheep as well. The difference, however, is whether or not we have a shepherd. Unbelievers, or the ungodly, are described in the Scripture as sheep without a shepherd.[2] Sheep are scattered, broken, and destitute without a good shepherd (Ezekiel 34:5). The sheep in this case do not simply sulk in their misery and brokenness, but rather seek to find rest. Sheep without a shepherd are endlessly searching for temporal things to heal their wounds and give them hope, but they wander—profiting from the world while losing their own souls. They search for peace, but do not find what they are looking for. Jesus was moved with compassion because the people were "harassed and helpless, like sheep without a shepherd" (Matthew 9:36).

Believers are different. Not different in our human experiences and not different in our description as sheep. We are different because we have a shepherd. Our shepherd sees our wounds and binds them. He sees when we stray and brings us back. He feeds us and leads us to green pastures and still waters. He lets us lie down and rest when we trust in him as our shepherd. Jesus does not simply put us at peace—he *is* our peace. He is our rest and the salve to heal our sheepishly wounded souls (Matthew 11:28–30). Let's go a little deeper into some of the ways Jesus has acted as our shepherd. It will give us much to contemplate and to rejoice in.

Savior Who Seeks the Lost

Jesus came to seek and to save those who are lost (Luke 19:10). Unbelievers who are dead, blind, hardened in heart—lost—need to be found. By grace Jesus came seeking the lost, to save those who are hostile toward him. What great love the Father demonstrates toward us that while we are still sinners Christ died for the ungodly (Romans 5:8). The Good Shepherd cares for souls by seeking the lost and praise him because he has found us! If Jesus went through the trouble to seek and save us, it makes sense that he would invest in our ongoing care through the work of the Holy Spirit and his Word.

The true shepherd of God also seeks after the straying sheep. "I will seek the lost," God said through the prophet Ezekiel, "and I will bring back the strayed, and I will bind up the injured, and I will strengthen the weak" (Ezekiel 34:16). Jesus demonstrated the character of a true shepherd by his teaching and by his life. In Matthew, Jesus told the parable of the lost sheep and asked rhetorically, "If a man has a hundred sheep, and one of them has gone astray, does he not leave the ninety-nine on the mountains and go in search of the one that went astray?" (Matthew 18:12). Seeking the lost and going after the strayed is a key characteristic of a shepherd and a key means by which Jesus demonstrates his care of souls. Martin Bucer said it this way,

Now, the pastoral ministry in the church has to be so extensive, in order that all the sheep should be sought out and brought into Christ's sheep-pen, and that those who have once come to Christ and into his sheep-pen, but have become strays and outcasts again, should be restored; similarly, that the injured should be healed, the diseased and weak strengthened, and the sleek and strong well protected and rightly shepherded.[3]

Jesus is not a hired hand. He has given himself. Laying down his life for his sheep proved that he is the Good Shepherd. The approval of God as seen in the resurrection validates his role as Chief Shepherd (1 Peter 5:4).

Jesus answered them, "I told you, and you do not believe. The works that I do in my Father's name bear witness about me, but you do not believe because you are not among my sheep. My sheep hear my voice, and I know them, and they follow me. I give them eternal life, and they will never perish, and no one will snatch them out of my hand. My Father, who has given them to me." (John 10:25–29)

Redeemer

Not only does Jesus shepherd our souls as our Savior, but also by his redemption. When human problems are described without reference to the curse of sin, the redemption of Christ is minimized or deemed unnecessary for our true healing. Conversely, when problems are explained through a biblical lens, individuals are dependent upon the mercies of Christ for help and hope—an uncomfortable position for proud, independent, wandering sheep. John Owen placed our dependence squarely upon Jesus when he said, "In particular, the Lord Christ is glorified in his repairing the violation of the glory of God in creation by sin. How beautifully ordered all things were as they lived and moved in dependence on God. But sin destroyed this order and harmony. But all is restored, repaired, and made up in this restoration of all things in our new head, Jesus Christ."[4]

Wonderful Counselor

Jesus also shepherds us with his counsel. He is our wonderful counselor. It is in him that all the treasures of wisdom and knowledge are found (Colossians 2:3). We are safe and secure from all alarms, because we are in Christ. We are able to live wisely because we are in the Beloved (Ephesians 1). To heed his counsel is to heed his Word. As the wonderful counselor, there is no sweeter words of wisdom by which to navigate our life than to be saturated by his word. Paul exhorts us, "Let the word of Christ dwell," because he knew that the wisdom of God is displayed in Christ (Colossians 3:16). The Word of Christ is his counsel to us.

To heed Christ's counsel is to love him. "If you love me," Jesus said, "you will keep my commandments" (John 14:15). The opposite is also true. Anyone who rejects the counsel of Christ is not neutral toward him. Those who reject his counsel reject Jesus himself. Jesus says it this way, "Whoever does not love me does not keep my words" (John 14:24). To obey Christ's words leads to life more abundant—a stable life, built upon the rock rather than shifting sand.

Heeding the counsel of Christ does not keep us from difficulty, but instead helps us walk at peace through suffering. Jesus does not ask the Father to take us out of the turmoil of the world, but to keep us from the evil one and sanctify us in truth (John 17:15–17). His word is the truth and we are guided by its counsel. Rejecting his counsel means we go astray and multiply brokenness. But his words are a balm to the broken and wounded soul. Jesus is our wonderful counselor, and his word is his wonderful counsel.

Conforms Us to His Image

The Good Shepherd is always at work in his sheep to conform us to his image. As the Word of God transforms our hearts, we are able to reflect the character of God. The word of God works in our heart to restore the fullness of the *imago dei* in us. A soul is mended and restored to its original design to the degree that it rests in faith upon the forgiveness God provides us in Jesus Christ. The heart then reflects the character of God as a display of his glory. This is the work of Christ, mender of the brokenhearted. The Holy Spirit works in us to transform us into the image of Christ, the one who reflected God perfectly on the earth.

This is the way God said it would be. The redeemed are to be conformed to the image of Christ (Romans 8:29). "We are predestined," Owen affirmed, "to be conformed to his image and it is this image that is produced in our souls by the power and virtue which comes from Christ."[5] Jesus is central because he is the true human. We are to be conformed to his image, because that is the way we were designed before the corruption of sin. As Owen said, "Christ communicates himself to us by creating a new nature, his own nature, in us."[6]

Why does Christ conform us to his image? God has not changed his goal for humanity. He created us in his image, and he is committed to transforming his people from one degree of glory to another (2 Corinthians 3:18). He desires to see the earth covered with his glory like the waters cover the sea (Habakkuk 2:14).

This goal has not been altered from the beginning. But sin corrupted it all. Sin entered the world through one man, and we all live differently from God's design because we are tainted by it. We experience untold difficulties which our own sins, the sins of others, and the sin cursed world all contribute to. Bodies decay and souls are blind. God's kindness in salvation is to heal our wounded souls, not only in our justification, but also through the sanctifying work of conforming us to the image of his Son—bringing us back to our design.

Jesus was the true human. He lived as God designed man to live, worshipping God with all his heart, soul, mind, and strength while loving his neighbor. He reflected the heart of God. He reflected the character of God. Paul said of Jesus, "He is the image of the invisible God" (Colossians 1:15). This is true health and life, and God has predestined that we who are his be refined to image him and reflect his glory.

As mentioned in chapter two, "A Biblical Vision for the Church as Culture of Care," in Jesus we now have an accurate picture of "normal." We can recognize what is normal and abnormal based upon how Jesus lived his life. Since the secular culture has no such way to delineate "normal," they struggle to categorize what is abnormal. We define normal humanity according to Jesus. Christianity has an aim, a focus, that we be conformed to his image. This implies that we are abnormal. It is an assumption that we need change, need help, and are desperately dependent upon God to be renewed back to fulfilling our purpose. As Lambert said, "In counseling, the only hope and help that matters in the long term is that which Jesus Christ brings."[7]

Sacrificially Loves Us

So how does our head and shepherd Jesus Christ treat us? He sacrificially loves us, washes us with his Word, nourishes us, and cherishes us as a husband his bride. Paul uses this metaphor to demonstrate the tender care of our Savior in Ephesians 5.

> . . . as Christ loved the church and gave himself up for her, that he might sanctify her, having cleansed her by the washing of water with the word, so that he might present the church to himself in splendor, without spot or wrinkle or any such thing, that she might be holy and without blemish. . . . For no one ever hated his own flesh, but nourishes and cherishes it, just as Christ does the church, because we are members of his body. (Ephesians 5:25b–27, 29–30)

He demonstrated his love by giving himself up for her. Jesus gave his life for us—not to gain a perfect bride, but a bride that he would need to be patient with and endure with as he sanctified her (us!).

Jesus sacrificed himself by giving up heaven to endure life in our cursed world. His daily endurance of trials and difficulties was a sacrifice he willingly gave to obtain a people for his possession. This culminated in the sacrifice we are most familiar with: his death on the cross. The love of Jesus was not lip service, but a demonstration of his love by giving himself sacrificially for us.

Washes Us with the Word

Our human nature typically expects something in return for our efforts. Jesus gave himself up for us so that he could give us more of himself. Jesus is patient with us. In our worst moments, he calls out to us to come to him so that he can tend our wounds and wash us with his Word. He aims to present us blameless to the Father, certainly by his righteousness imputed to us, but also by sanctifying us. Jesus washes us with the Word so that we can become in practice what we have been declared in the truth of our justification.

As we wrestle in this body of death with the world, the flesh, and the devil, and the boastful pride of life, it is the Word of God that washes us clean. It's significant that the tool Jesus uses to wash our conscience clean is his Word. So Jesus endures, patiently washing us with his Word to cleanse us and make us like himself. This tells us something of the character of Christ—he is gentle—and of the effective work of his Word in us.

Feeds and Nourishes Us

What does his Word do in us? His Word cleanses us and also nourishes our souls. When the body is nourished it cannot stagnate. Growth and maturity are the aim and outcome of nourishment. In fact, the word used in Ephesians 5 translated as "nourish" means to sustain and to mature. The way we are sustained and matured is to be nourished by Christ as he applies his Word to our hearts. This type of care is by God's design, but it reveals the heart of Christ for his people. He tenderly cares and nourishes us so that we are sustained through life.

As our shepherd, Jesus feeds his flock by giving us himself. He feeds our souls by the nourishment of his Word. It sustains and grows us to become more like him. We grow in maturity by feeding upon the principles and precepts of every word that proceeds from the mouth of God.

Remember the progression of John 6? The scene begins with Jesus feeding the five thousand. Then, after the story of Jesus walking on water, the next section is one of our Lord's "I am" declarations. Jesus said, "I am the bread of life" (John 6:35). Jesus had filled the bellies of his hearers, but now he is describing how they can partake of him and be filled forever. Using the provision of manna from heaven as a foreshadowing, Jesus said, "Truly, truly, I say to you, it was not Moses who gave you the bread from heaven, but my Father gives you the true bread from heaven. For the bread of God is he who comes down from heaven and gives life to the world" (John 6:32–33). Jesus went on to say that anyone who ate of this bread of God from heaven would never hunger. Many around him were asking questions, so he clarified what he meant.

> Truly, truly, I say to you, unless you eat the flesh of the Son of Man and drink his blood, you have no life in you. Whoever feeds on my flesh and drinks my blood has eternal life, and I will raise him up on the last day. For my flesh is true food, and my blood is true drink. Whoever feeds on my flesh and drinks my blood abides in me, and I in him. As the living Father sent me, and I live because of the Father, so whoever feeds on me, he also will live because of me. This is the bread that came down from heaven, not like the bread the fathers ate, and died. Whoever feeds on this bread will live forever. (John 6:53–58)

Jesus is giving us further revelation regarding the good pasture that God provides through his true shepherd. The good food is to partake of Christ himself. Jesus shepherds us by guiding us to good pastures of himself.

Pause for a moment and focus on the journey God has brought you through, and remember God's kindness. Even through all of your difficulty and suffering, he has allowed you to taste of the good pastures of Christ. To trust in him and follow him means that all of our suffering is meaningful. He is helping us to turn from our appetite for temporal things, so that we may eat of the true bread of Christ and live. He does not treat us like the bad shepherds who use and abuse the sheep for their own selfish gain. He loves and cherishes his flock and guides them into good pasture to find food so that the sheep may grow and flourish and walk in peace with God (Ezekiel 34:14).

Cherishes Us

The cold that leaks down into your bones is so hard to warm back up. Nothing feels better on your frozen feet than to prop them up on a fireplace with the warmth of the fire helping to thaw the cold. This is similar imagery to the meaning of Jesus, who nourishes and *cherishes* his body.

He warms us with his care. Tenderly he fosters the care of our souls, which warms the heart of our inner man. To be cherished by another human being is one thing, but to be cherished by the Creator of the universe is something entirely all its own. The affectionate care of Jesus warms the heart which kindles a flame that burns brightly and passionately for his glory. There is no fear in love, and to know that Christ cherishes his body and shepherds our souls is an encouragement and comfort in the darkest of times.

Heals the Broken[8]

Sin, both original and personal, is the reason for the brokenness of us and our world. The first sin of Adam and Eve that resulted in the brokenness of the whole world was their rejection of God's word. The crafty serpent asked our first parents, "Did God actually say . . . ?" (Genesis 3:1). That small speck of doubt, and the action they took based upon it, caused the groaning of all creation. But it was at that moment that Christ was promised as the seed who would come to crush the cause of our brokenness (Genesis 3:15). His purpose was to glorify the Father, and it pleased the Father to be glorified through crushing the iniquity that caused the brokenness.

God has not forgotten the brokenhearted. Rather, he has demonstrated his care by sending Christ to bandage and heal those who have been broken. Jesus was the long-awaited one who came to crush the curse of sin and death. In Jeremiah 8, the shepherds of Israel were unsuccessful in healing the brokenness of God's people. The chapter concludes with a series of rhetorical questions: "Is there no balm in Gilead? Is there no physician there? Why then has the health of the daughter of my people not been restored?" (Jeremiah 8:22). God was revealing that the remedy for the broken heart is to be found in the "balm in Gilead." Jesus, as the fulfillment of Isaiah 61, is the one who binds the brokenhearted; he is the medicinal balm that heals the wounded heart. Matthew Henry states that "The blood of Christ is balm in Gilead, his Spirit is the physician there, both sufficient, all-sufficient."[9]

Strengthens the Weak

Do you delight in your weakness? We typically try to hide our weaknesses. In most cultures weaknesses are so named because they are a hindrance to success. But Christians need not hide or run from their weaknesses. As Paul did, Christians may "boast" in their weaknesses so that Christ would be made strong.

Jesus strengthens the weak. This is a primary duty displayed in his shepherding. Christ is made perfect in us by demonstrating his strength in spite of our weaknesses. Jesus said to Paul, "My grace is sufficient for you, for my power is made perfect in weakness" (2 Corinthians 12:9).

The discussion in the Scripture related to this topic is not focused so much on our weaknesses but on the strength of Christ. Our weaknesses are front and center so that we refrain from boasting in ourselves. What a kindness of God to keep us from foolishly trusting in our weaknesses. Instead, he reveals them so we may embrace them humbly, and so that Christ can be perfected in us. The result? We see the power of Christ and boast in him alone. We can trust his tender care as a shepherd who strengthens the weak. We know that we can invite those who have weaknesses to find the strength that is to be found *in Christ* alone because he alone strengthens the weak.

Makes the Flock Rest

True rest is found in Jesus. This does not mean that once you become a Christian that your life is now lived on "easy street." Our souls may truly rest in Christ because he has made peace between us and God. Jesus himself is our peace (Ephesians 2:14). Peace and rest are not to be found in a feeling, but in a person. They are not to be found at a simple moment in time, but in a position. We who are in Christ are at peace with God (Romans 5:1). It is because we are found in Christ that we may enjoy the rest he has prepared for us.

Our shepherd has provided peace for us and guides us by quiet waters. He makes us to lie down in green pastures. The goodness of our shepherd makes his flock to rest. As our high priest, he has done the work to appease the wrath of God, and now we can be at peace and rest. We cannot make atonement by our religious busyness; Christ has provided our rest. Yet we need to follow the Good Shepherd because his work and care have made us to rest.

Protects the Flock

Jesus seeks the lost and goes after the stray sheep, but even more that that he protects the flock. He is no hired hand who does not risk his life for the sheep in danger. Jesus is the door to the sheepfold. He has put himself between us—his church—and the wrath of God. He has protected us and he continues that work. Nothing will pluck us from his hand.

He protects the flock by guarding our hearts with his peace that surpasses comprehension (Philippians 4:7). As the Good Shepherd, Jesus protects us from our sinful desires. He empowers us to overcome our fears, doubts, and temptations. Jesus protects his flock from fiery darts, the cares of this world, and ultimately eternal death. Jesus is the Good Shepherd who protects the flock given to him.

How the Sheep Should Respond to the Shepherd?

Listen to His Voice

One of the most satisfying things in life is hearing beautiful sounds—a bird singing, an orchestra playing, the ocean crashing. The skill of musicians who have perfected their craft is a delight to the ear. As I am writing this book, I am listening to music in the background. Its beauty calms and soothes me.

As a father, the voice of your child calling out to you is one of the most endearing sounds. It is an amazing thing to be in a crowded and noisy space and hear the call of your child. You know their voice and it hits your ears differently, distinct from all other sounds. How much more soothing is it to our ears and calming to our minds to hear the voice of our loving shepherd? How much more should our ears be tuned to hear the voice of our Lord above all of the noises in our world?

> Jesus answered them, "I told you, and you do not believe. The works that I do in my Father's name bear witness about me, but you do not believe because you are not among my sheep. My sheep hear my voice, and I know them, and they follow me. I give them eternal life, and they will never perish, and no one will snatch them out of my hand. My Father, who has given them to me, is greater than all, and no one is able to snatch them out of the Father's hand." (John 10:25–29)

Our daily prayer should be: "Lord, tune our ear to hear your voice; tune our will to obey your commands; tune our hearts to sing your praises." The sheep of Christ listen to his voice. By that I do not mean that Jesus is speaking audibly and that my physical ears hear the Good Shepherd. Hebrews 1:1–2 says, "Long ago, at many times and in many ways, God spoke to our fathers by the prophets, but in these last days he has spoken to us by his Son, whom he appointed the heir of all things, through whom he also created the world." God speaks to us through his Word—the written, living Word. The sheep must know his voice and listen, not simply to be hearers but to respond by doing. We know his voice and we follow him because we listen to him.

Depend on Him

The proper disposition of sheep is dependence upon the shepherd. John Owen places our dependence squarely upon Jesus when he said, "In particular, the Lord Christ is glorified in his repairing the violation of the glory of

God in creation by sin. How beautifully ordered all things were as they lived and moved in dependence on God. But sin destroyed this order and harmony. But all is restored, repaired, and made up in this restoration of all things in our new head, Jesus Christ."[10] Not only *can* we trust and depend on Christ as a faithful shepherd, we *must* put the full weight of our dependence upon him. One of the reasons life is difficult is because we must constantly be learning to crush our natural self-reliance and walk in faith, trusting the Good Shepherd.

Depending on Christ does not keep us from difficulties, but helps us walk at peace through suffering. Jesus does not ask the Father to take us out of the turmoil of the world, but to keep us from the evil one and sanctify us in truth (John 17:15–17). As we trust in Jesus, we can join with the psalmist and declare, "Even though I walk through the valley of the shadow of death, I will fear no evil, for you are with me" (Psalm 23:4).

Discussion Questions

1. List some of the ways that Jesus shows himself to be the Good Shepherd of his people, the church.
2. How is Jesus shepherding you right now? How do you see him shepherding your church right now?
3. Name the ways we are to respond to Christ's shepherding of us.
4. Which of these responses do you need to grow most in? Which of these responses does your church need to grow most in?

CHAPTER SIX

The Care of Under-Shepherds

Twenty-five and newly minted from seminary, I began my first day as an associate pastor. I was excited and full of plans, but deep down I also was wrestling with how clueless I was about ministry. I arrived on the first day of the job to begin arranging my new office. I had big plans for this office. As I approached the door, I wasn't quite prepared for what I found. An older gentleman from the church was sitting on the floor of my office. On the floor with him was a box of furniture pieces that would eventually be my desk.

Sam was a decorated military veteran. His presence demanded respect; he intimidated most folks he was around simply by his reputation and no-nonsense personality. Yet, there he sat—on the floor—prepared to serve me, a young pastor fresh out of seminary. I don't think I appreciated the magnitude of this moment when it was happening, but his service and words during that day, and many subsequent conversations afterward, left an indelible mark on me. I had been taught the theology behind pastoral ministry, but I underestimated the privilege and weighty responsibility given to the office.

He hadn't prepared a Bible lesson for that day, but in the ensuing moments he taught me a great deal about pastoral ministry. His first move was to stand up, almost at attention, as he shook my hand and greeted me. He said, "Welcome, pastor," with a warm smile and focused eyes that conveyed respect for the office. I'm sure he had many other things he could have been doing, but here he was, spending his retirement by taking his place on the floor to serve me. His willingness to serve me resounded like a megaphone in my mind as he demonstrated a little of the heart of pastoral care.

The second thing I have long thought about was the way he addressed me. I was twenty-five and inexperienced, yet Sam addressed me as pastor. I had not done anything in particular to deserve that title, and I should have been the one saluting him, but Sam respected how the Word of God set apart the role of a pastor and his ministry. He respected the office to which God had called me, and he emphasized that respect by referring to me with the title of "pastor." Rather than swelling with pride, his comment that day helped me to feel a proper sense of the burden of pastoral ministry like nothing I had felt before. The Lord was bringing together my education with real life in a profound way, to help me consider more deeply the role of a shepherd and how the shepherd is to care for his flock. The burden I felt that day was not the weight of a ball and chain; instead it was a sense of the high calling of caring for God's people and a passion to fulfill that calling.

Shepherd the Flock of God

We often use the language of shepherding to describe that high calling, but what does that really mean? Do we mean that elders are to give sound advice? Do we mean every elder should get some sort of professional counseling degree in order to care for the church? We should not reduce the role of shepherding to merely being a figurehead who makes a few decisions but does not interact with the sheep except for rare occasions, and never in too close proximity. But neither should we expand it to demand that he fit the world's category of competence in order to address the soulish problems of life with a professionalized counseling degree.

A crucial statement regarding shepherding care is found in Hebrews 13:17. The author of Hebrews said, "Obey your leaders and submit to them, for they are keeping watch over your souls, as those who will have to give an account. Let them do this with joy and not with groaning, for that would be of no advantage to you." The writer encouraged pastors, consistently with other passages in the New Testament, to keep watch over souls. Paul told the Ephesian elders to "pay careful attention . . . to care for the church of God" (Acts 20:28). He raised the value of this task by describing how the sheep became the church of God, reminding them that Christ "obtained [them] with his own blood."

Elders are called to shepherd on behalf of Christ for his people. This is the flock Christ secured with his own blood. He bore shame and sorrow to care for sinners. He sympathizes with us because he became like us in every way. Elders are responsible to care for souls in the same way as Jesus gave himself to care for souls. Reformer Martin Bucer agreed, saying, "Therefore it has pleased him [Jesus] to exercise his rule, protection and care of us who are still in this world with and through the ministry of his word, which he does so outwardly through his ministers and instruments."[1]

We are his hands and feet to offer the wisdom of God and compassionate care, guiding sheep through this valley of the shadow of death, home to their Savior and Lord.

When pastors hear teaching on biblical counseling, they often raise a concern of burnout with the responsibilities they already carry. Even when they are convinced of the principles behind biblical counseling, they wonder if they can add counseling to their other responsibilities. This is one of the reasons why it is so important to reshape our view of "professionalized" pastoral ministry. Some Christians think (even if they don't say it out loud) that because the pastor is paid to do the work of the ministry, he should be the one doing *all* of the ministry. In reality, our church-as-business models have placed us in a corner, forcing us to think that since pastoral staff is paid, they are the experts or professionals and the only ones intended to do ministry. While pastors should be leading and modeling this type of ministry among their people, every Christian is called to minister to each other and bear the burdens of one another as we are conformed to the image of Christ. How does that happen? The under-shepherds are called to equip the saints for the work of the ministry. This is one primary way to build a culture of care in your church, and we will unpack this more in the next chapter.

The office of elder is crucial to the flourishing of the church as a culture of care. The church is made up of broken people who need to grow in maturity, and God provides them with shepherds to minister his Word in order to make them complete in Christ. And yet, today it seems as though the position of elder is seen more as a professional preacher or administrator rather than as shepherd.[2] It is inarguable that shepherding in American churches has diminished at least to some degree.[3] But God has uniquely structured the church for the care of souls and the role of the elder is crucial in leading the church culture. The tasks given to shepherds in the Scripture demonstrate that the church is designed to care for those struggling with sin or broken by suffering.

Shepherding is not a neutral task. There are consequences to how an elder shepherds. It is a bit like what we say when talking about theology, "Everyone is a theologian;

some are just really bad theologians." The same is true when speaking of elders. Every elder is a shepherd, but some are not very good ones. Many elders defer shepherding duties to others, but that decision is not neutral—it has negative effects on the sheep (i.e., Jeremiah 6; Jeremiah 8; Ezekiel 34). Thus, every elder must seriously consider what shepherding entails and endeavor by the grace of God to be faithful in fulfilling those duties.

My goal in this section is not to burden the conscience of any pastor with additional requirements that go beyond God's Word. Furthermore, this chapter is not an exhaustive treatment of the qualifications and responsibilities of elders and deacons; many other excellent books have been written on this topic.[4] I simply want elders to ask the following questions as they relate to the care of souls: What am I responsible for? What does God require? For what will God hold me accountable?

However, before we can begin discussing what elders are to *do* in regard to soul care, it's important to briefly remind elders of who they *are* in their role as elders. The first thing elders must remember is that while they are shepherds of the church, their true status is that of under-shepherds serving the purposes of the Chief Shepherd of the church, Jesus Christ. MacArthur helpfully points out, "The elder acts as a caring and loving shepherd over the flock but never in Scripture is it spoken of as 'his flock,' or 'your flock.' It is the 'flock of God' (1 Peter 5:2), and he is merely a steward—a caretaker over the possession of God."[5] Christians do not follow men, but Christ (Acts 5:29; 1 Corinthians 3:21–23). Jesus is the head and chief shepherd. Pastors are to be stewards—shepherding the *flock of God* by imitating how Christ shepherds his people.

Concerning Trends

As mentioned in chapter five, "Christ as Our Good Shepherd," Jeremiah 6 and 8 reveal the inadequacies and dangers of human shepherds. But now our Good Shepherd has appeared. And he is still ruling, reigning, and helping his church. He gives elders to the church so that soul care can be accomplished in his name, in his way, through dependence on his Spirit and the Word.

To shepherd the church Christ's way, the pastoral office is crucial. Without shepherds the church cannot function as a culture of care. Pastoral duties coincide with the purpose for which God gave the church he is to serve. This is why it is so troubling that more and more of the shepherding work of the church has been professionalized and often outsourced.

As discussed earlier, while pastors were once viewed as physicians of the soul, today their work is seen more as a professional preacher or administrator only.[6] That the task of shepherding has been diminished is a well-documented reality.[7] Notice David Wells's observations:

> Pastors once believed that they were called to think about life, to think in ways that were centered in and disciplined by the truth of God's Word, although, as Tocqueville observed, there has always been a tendency latent in the American soul to think of religion in terms of its utility rather than its truth. Modernity has now exaggerated this tendency to the extent that the older ways of understanding the pastor's responsibilities are disappearing, along with the older ideas about training pastors for their work. As the technological world has encroached upon the pastorate, management by technique has come to replace management by the truth. . . . And

so the professionalized pastor has often reduced the uncontrollable world of God's truth by procedure, using committees to diminish the church and psychological techniques to diminish the soul.[8]

In order to reclaim the role of the elder in soul care, it is critical to understand the structure of the church with Jesus as our head and shepherd. The elders operate as under-shepherds, whom God has uniquely gifted, called, and equipped under the authority and structure of the church to care of souls. The care of the broken is intrinsically built within God's design of the church, which is clearly demonstrated by the tasks he gives to the shepherds who lead his people.

Let's look specifically at the responsibility given to the men God has called to lead his church through the lens of how Jesus, as our Good Shepherd, cares for the flock of God. Although elders are certainly quite different from our perfect Savior, we are uniquely called to imitate him in these ways as his under-shepherds. These are not all of the duties of elders, but they provide a helpful way to look at the role of elder specifically as it relates to soul care.

Keep Watch

No one really likes to admit that they might need shepherding, but remember: sheep need to be shepherded. American individualism makes shepherding even more of a countercultural idea. But we are sheep, according to Scripture, and we need our Good Shepherd and the men he has appointed to be his under-shepherds. I am not suggesting that we abandon our personal responsibility to Christ. We are governed by Christ; we are a priesthood of believers with Christ as our chief shepherd. Yet, God ordained his church to have overseers with responsibilities to "keep watch" over us.

The elder is to minister to Christ's people using his counsel, the Word. He is to speak this truth, in love, guard this truth with his life and reputation, and pray diligently that the flock walk in this truth. These elements are a part of his proverbial shepherd's staff to guide, guard, protect, and comfort the flock of God entrusted to him. Remember that according to Hebrews 13:17 and Acts 20:28, that God has entrusted to elders, the under-shepherds of his church the care of the souls in their church. They are to do this by "keeping watch" and "paying careful attention."

What we think it means for pastors and elders to keep watch and pay careful attention to the flock under their care has wide-reaching implications for our current practice of soul care within the church. Sadly, for more than a century, most pastoral students in seminary have received very little training regarding their duty to pay careful attention or keep watch over the souls of the people entrusted to them. It seems to me that since pastors will be held responsible by God for how they do this task, it would be vital to understand what this means. Is God requiring that they simply preach a biblical sermon every week? That is a good start, but it doesn't quite seem to grasp the diligence involved or the magnitude required to *keep watch*. The phrase implies biblical shepherding in the sense that the eyes of the elders are keen and in constant vigilance toward the good of the sheep. They are motivated to do so by love for God, love for the sheep, and a desire to give a good account to God and of their care for the sheep.

For some pastors, the care of souls means only preaching their Sunday sermon; for others it is meeting once with a troubled person, then referring them to someone else. Others may go so far as to hire staff to take this responsibility. I would encourage pastors to look beyond what has been the cultural norm for the last century and contemplate what the responsibility to pay careful attention to the flock entails.

The distance many pastors keep from their flock makes this task nearly impossible. A given in the shepherding of real (not metaphorical) sheep is that you will get messy and muddy working with them. If we are as deeply engaged with our flock as this image suggests, then we will be constantly forced to be dependent upon God's wisdom to help those in need. Many of us do not like this type of vulnerability, but it is best for us and for our people. Pierre and Reju remind us, "A pastor who labors lightly among his people often labors lightly before God. . . . The misery of the world is often what prompts the prayers of God's people."[9] As shepherds when we see the misery of people under our care it should move us to pray with and for them and to move toward them in love.

Let's walk through some specific ways that pastors and elders are called as under-shepherds to "keep watch" and "pay attention" as Jesus does in his care for our souls.

Protect the Flock

One use of the shepherd's staff was to protect the flock from danger. Obviously the staff would be used to fight off wolves and other predators to keep the flock safe. The staff would also be used to rescue the sheep from danger of their own making. The crook could function as a lasso to snatch the shepherd's possession from muck and mire or crevices where sheep had fallen. Used to keep danger away from without or to protect from self-induced harm, the staff was a handy tool for the shepherd. Caring well for the flock is not only mending the broken, but guarding them from vain philosophies and empty deceptions.

The Word of God is the staff of the under-shepherds of God's flock. The Word is one tool, but it is not always used in the same way. The situation calls for different uses of the staff, but the common goal in all circumstances is to protect the flock from external enemies and from harm caused by our own sin.

Make the Flock Rest

The staff of the shepherd is used to guide the sheep into the sheep pen where they would be safe for rest. Jesus is the Good Shepherd who is the door of the sheepfold. Elders are able to remind the sheep of the Good Shepherd who has done the work that is worthy of their salvation. We are not able to work our way into favor with God. Good shepherds lead their flock to rest in the finished work of Christ.

On a more "practical" level, elders take time for sabbath rest each week because they know that their identity is not in their accomplishments but in what Christ has done for them. So elders are able to model true rest in the work of Christ in order to teach the flock not only in their words of teaching, but in their deeds as well.

Pastors so often work themselves into the ground, as if there is no place for rest. I am certainly not encouraging laziness in the pastorate. But too many pastors and congregations do not practically live as if the work of Jesus on their behalf is finished. Elders lead by example and should be first in demonstrating the urgency of the work of ministry. However, elders should also lead by example in shepherding the flock to rest in Christ, who is our sabbath (Matthew 12:8).

Feed the Flock

In the same way the staff was used to guide the sheep to rest, it is used to guide the sheep to food. The staff of the elder actually supersedes this metaphor, because the same Word of God that guides is the same Word that nourishes his people. The elders feed the flock by faithfully proclaiming the Word.

The duty of the elder is to feed the sheep, not feed *upon* the sheep. To feed upon the sheep is to use them for selfish ambition or greedy gain. Elders are to imitate Christ and serve him by pouring themselves out to nourish and cherish the sheep (Jeremiah 8; Ezekiel 34; Ephesians 5). The food elders serve which most nourishes the soul is the Word. The sufficient Word of God revives the soul, enlightens the eyes, makes the simple wise, and rejoices the heart (Psalm 119:7–10). These are not the meals our flesh craves, but it is the nourishment we need. Elders are to be faithful in feeding the flock corporately and personally.

Strengthen the Weak

Our human frailty is exposed more often than we care to admit. Our weaknesses abound, but our culture presses us to look inside ourselves for answers and strength. The cultural narrative appeals to our flesh, but it actually exacerbates our weaknesses rather than cures them. Our strength is found in the strength of another: our Lord Jesus.

The responsibility was given to Jesus as our shepherd to strengthen the weak (Ezekiel 34:11–19).[10] He continues that work as the Holy Spirit uses his sword and the labor of his under-shepherds to strengthen us in the inner person. We are to proclaim the promises of God, which have been made sure and "more" convincing in the person of Jesus and through the atonement that he made behind the veil. His atonement was not offered in a tent or temple made with human hands, but in the very presence of God. It is this promise of Christ that is a sure "anchor of our soul"

(Hebrews 6:19). As the winds and waves of the turbulent world toss our hearts to and fro, we have an anchor that strengthens our resolve.

Elders have been called to proclaim this sure and true strength to our weak and vulnerable souls.

There are two basic ways elders neglect shepherding the weaknesses of the sheep. The first is that elders practically accept culturally preferable ways as means of strength. We do this by promoting the empty philosophies of humanistic psychology, which advocate for the strengthening of the self as a primary means for health. A second way is the simple neglect to promote trust, hope, and obedience in the Word of God as the primary means for our soul's delight.

The silence of elders on these destructive worldly strategies does not strengthen the sheep, but makes them vulnerable to drift toward the empty deceptions of the world. In these cases, elders are not strengthening the weak but leading them to glory in their own strength. Trusting in ourselves is our greatest human weakness, yet we have been deceived into believing it is our means to strength. Human hearts and human flesh will fail. Elders must consistently remind God's people that God is their true strength. The psalmist declared, "My flesh and my heart may fail, but God is the strength of my heart and my portion forever" (Psalm 73:26). Elders strengthen the weak by the strength found in Christ alone. Paul found this not only helpful but necessary for his weaknesses, and God's grace in Christ will be found sufficient in all of our frailties in the same way his grace was sufficient for the apostle (2 Corinthians 12:9).

Heal the Broken

As we saw in the previous chapter, the work of Jesus our shepherd is to heal the brokenhearted. Under-shepherds should feel the inadequacy this task demands. In fact, many elders feel the weight of this responsibility and prefer someone else to do this work. But the work of a shepherd, as demonstrated by Christ, is to heal the wounds of the broken.

What makes the difference for elders is the tool we use to bring about this inner healing. We are called to point the flock to the Great Physician, Jesus. Elders are called upon to appropriately apply the salve of his Word to the need of the moment. We are called to pray for the sick so they may be healed (James 5:14). We are taught to grow the inner man, even while the outer man is wasting away (2 Corinthians 4:7).

Elders are certainly not medical professionals. We do not preclude or deter anyone from proper medical attention. Modern medical care is a common grace given to us. But even with the amazing advancements in curative medicine, all of that good is only a foreshadowing of the true redemption and healing believers find fully in Christ. Elders point others to Christ who, at his second coming, will heal and redeem once and for all every ailment, in both body and soul.

Seek the Lost and Wandering

The "seeker-friendly" church as it has been described is, according to the Bible, a misnomer. "None is righteous, no, not one; no one understands; no one seeks for God" (Romans 3:10–11). It is not the unbeliever who is the seeker, but the elders who are the seekers. They are to seek the same thing that Jesus came to seek: "For the Son of Man came to seek and to save the lost" (Luke 19:10). Elders are to lead in demonstrating the urgency of seeking the lost and broken with the gospel.

Our mission to share the good news of Christ is one primary way the church is commissioned to care for souls. Evangelism is one way we learn to lay down our own lives—putting aside our fears and concern of reputation—for the sake of another, so that they may have their hearts of stone be turned into hearts of flesh (Ezekiel 36:26). Evangelism is deep soul care which takes engagement in spiritual warfare for the good of another so that they may have life abundant and eternal.

Since Jesus Christ is preeminent over all things, he could have made another way for his gospel to go forward into the world. The gospel was born in the suffering of Jesus. It will continue its proclamation by the sufferings of his people. Humans come to faith—are made alive—by hearing the Word (Romans 10:9–10). God spoke and the world was created, but he chose the foolishness of his preached Word to awaken dead hearts. I suppose he could have ordained any number of means, but that is not the way.

Jesus took Gethsemane's cup and endured the cross because there was no other way. Paul endured all sorts of hardships because there was no other way. Missionaries have endured untold suffering because there is no other way. Pastors have endured the pressures of shepherding broken and sometimes recalcitrant sheep, because there is no other way. We teach our people to overcome their fears and to share the gospel with their neighbors because there is no other way.

More powerful than nuclear bombs or the engine of rocket ships, the proclamation of God's Word by the work of the Holy Spirit does the miraculous. And for what reason? So that Christ will receive glory in the Spirit's giving life. So that we would not boast in any other thing or name for the saving of our souls. "For by grace you have been saved through faith. And this is not of yourselves . . . so that no one may boast" (Ephesians 2:8–9). There is no other name under heaven by which people are saved (Acts 4:12). There is no greater anchor for our soul as the torrents of life billow than the assurance of our salvation in Christ. It is a sure and steady hope in which we should always take refuge (Psalm 46:1–2).

Corporate Proclamation

The way Jesus cares for his people is imitated by the way elders shepherd the flock of God among them. In the same way that the Word of God, as the shepherd's staff, is used to protect and guide the flock, the way in which elders shepherd with the Word is in both the corporate and personal ministry of the Word. Notice that the situation may change, but the means of ministry does not. The Word of God remains the constant shepherd's staff, but it is used in different ways for the need of the moment for the good of the sheep. Corporate proclamation and personal ministry of the Word should be the means by which we accomplish the shepherding tasks just described. The environment of the shepherding may shift between public and private, but the means of ministry by the Word does not alter.

The preaching ministry of the Word of God is vital to the health of the local body. Time dedicated to corporate care may be the most important hour of our week. Every member of the body tunes their ear to hear the Word of God through God's servant as he labors to proclaim the counsel of God. It is here that we are nourished. We feed upon the bread of God, and our hearts are encouraged.

The clear and consistent proclamation of God's inspired and authoritative Word has its due effects upon hearers. The return on the Word faithfully preached brings about a range of responses that are normal and good works of the Holy Spirit. The Word edifies and strengthens our hearts, it soothes with comfort in desperate times, and illuminates by sharp conviction sin rooted in the dark crevices of our hearts. The function of preaching God's Word is intended as a means to care for our souls. Week in and week out we have burdens, need to be renewed in the spirit of our mind, and need to seek the Lord in repentance.

The preached Word is a ministry of care for our souls. The elders labor to minister these words of comfort and conviction, and the Spirit of God applies it appropriately to the ear that hears. Paul reminds us, "the word of the cross is folly to those who are perishing, but to us who are being saved it is the power of God. . . . [W]e preach Christ crucified, a stumbling block to Jews and folly to Gentiles, but to those who are called, both Jews and Greeks, Christ the power of God and the wisdom of God" (1 Corinthians 1:18, 23–24). Notice that the cross of Christ is not simply for justification; it is for us who are *being saved*. The Word ministers to our hearts at various points of need to care for our souls.

As the Bible is faithfully preached, the hearts of God's people are not only encouraged but exposed. Those things once hidden become evident; our thoughts and intentions thriving in deception are discerned and brought to light (Jeremiah 17:9; Hebrews 4:12–13). This effect of preaching demands more intimate ministry of the Word. Shepherding certainly happens corporately in pulpit ministry, but it must not end there. Sheep need individual care. Mass vaccinations may be appropriate as preventative care, but they are lousy treatments for individual wounds.

Personal Ministry

I agree with Pierre and Reju that "We are not calling into question the primacy of the preaching ministry. We are merely pointing out that it is not the only place that the ministry of the Word happens in the life of the church."[11] If we limit the ministry of the Word to the pulpit, intentional or not, the care of the sheep is lacking.

When Paul tells elders to "Pay careful attention to yourselves and to all the flock," he was not referring only to the public ministry of the Word (Acts 20:28). Paying careful attention must mean more than making sure you have delivered a biblical and well-crafted sermon. The care of Jesus was not simply done from heaven. He came in flesh and dwelt among us. He was near us, walking our streets, breathing our air, eating our food. His ministry was done by public proclamation and personal interactions. It may be said that Jesus did as much or more counseling ministry as public proclamation. I do not mean to say counseling and personal ministry are *more important*. My point is to say that both are necessary. If we are to shepherd God's flock the way the great Shepherd did, then we must minister the word of God up close and personal. Jesus did ministry seeing the whites of people's eyes, and our shepherding should replicate that proximity and care for the sheep.

Personal ministry of the Word makes sense for pastors who believe in expository ministry. If elders believe that the preaching of the Word, even though foolish to the world, is effectual in the hearts of the hearers by the Holy Spirit, then it makes sense that we would also believe the same about the personal ministry of the Word of God. These settings bring greater opportunity for more specific application of the Word than can usually be shared in a corporate setting. When you are speaking one-to-one with someone, you are hearing their specific story, their specific hurts or burdens. The Holy Spirit is present in those situations as well—giving you compassion, insight, and just the right words from the Bible for the need of the moment.

Many pastors feel inadequate for the work of counseling. But we should not let a cultural requirement of professionalism define what is necessary for the task of soul care. "[T]he task of caring has been given into the hands of other professionals. The advent of the secular therapist and the explosion of the social services has meant that pastors often are made to feel like amateurs among professionals, with little to contribute to the problems of the real world."[12] That is not to dismiss training and growing in skill, but to redirect what is most important in caring. Our sufficiency is in Christ. We are called to give the wisdom of God as "servants of Christ and stewards of the mysteries of God. Moreover, it is required of stewards that they be found faithful" (1 Corinthians 4:1–2). Pierre and Reju encourage pastors that "any sense of inadequacy in counseling should not be reason to avoid it; rather, it should keep you dependent upon God to do what he alone can do."[13] It is an uncomfortable place to be, but it is the healthiest place for us to be as we minister to God's flock.

The Work of the Spirit

All elders should feel inadequate for the tasks we have been called to perform as shepherds. In ourselves, we do not have what it takes to accomplish the work of the ministry. We are dependent upon the grace of Christ and the work of the Holy Spirit.

But thankfully, Jesus is present in the church as head and shepherd. The Scripture tells us that Jesus is in heaven, so how does he carry out his duties as head and shepherd of his church? He cares for us who are still in the world by the ministry of the Spirit and Word. Christ has given us his Spirit to know and understand the Word of God— the counsel of Jesus. The Holy Spirit testifies of Christ so that our Lord changes us into his image. This process brought about by the work of the Spirit through the Word of God helps us to live in practice according to the truth that Christ is our head. The Spirit of God regenerates us, bringing us to life in Christ. The Spirit illuminates the Word and guides us into all truth (John 14:26; 16:7–11; 1 Corinthians 2:2; Galatians 5:16–26). The Spirit convicts of sin according to the Word and frees us from its bondage (2 Corinthians 3:12–18). The Spirit teaches and sanctifies us to the praise and glory of Christ. The Spirit provides guidance, but not apart from his sword, the Word of God. All of this work is not neutral to our souls. This is the work of Christ as head and shepherd. He cares for our souls by providing the Spirit and his Word.

The work of the Spirit of God in the counseling room is the way in which Christ personally shepherds his people. In biblical counseling the work of the Spirit is necessary because he is the agent of change. By design, Christ said that the Spirit would "sanctify them in the truth; your word is truth" (John 17:17). So it makes sense for us to minister the Word as the Sword of the Spirit, to shepherd the souls of Christ's sheep.

Deacons

There are full-length books and wonderful commentaries addressing the role and responsibilities of deacons.[14] I want to highlight just a few to stir your thinking about their role in relationship to soul care. Deacons are required to have the same character qualifications as the elder, in part because they are viewed as leaders of God's church, but also because in caring for others deacons must be trustworthy servants. So much pain and heartache have come from untrustworthy leaders using their position to feed on the sheep rather than care for them. The qualifications of the deacon are equally important because the care they offer is to people who are in need and vulnerable.

The office of deacon demonstrates the emphasis God places upon the care of his people. Deacons play a key role in the care of souls as they focus on care for those in physical need.[15] When I say that the church is responsible for soul care, I am not saying that we are only souls. I am simply acknowledging that the heart is the center of our being. The role of deacons demonstrates that God cares for the whole person through his church.

Deacons are to serve the body so that the elders maintain focus upon ministering the Word and prayer. These tasks were to be guarded because they are vital to the health of a church. Elders are to maintain primary focus on the spiritual needs of the body. So often in our modern culture, ministry of the Word of God, the work of the Holy Spirit, and prayer are downplayed as inadequate and insufficient means to care for people. We tend to think that modern advances have made irrelevant the supernatural dependence of Christians upon God. The role of deacon, however, helps us to understand that God views prayer and ministry of the Word to be vital. Deacons were called to guard and protect the focus of prayer and ministry of the word for elders.

The work of the elder in caring for souls is necessary, the Word is sufficient, and human beings must live deeply dependent upon God through prayer. Yet, God does not devalue the physical needs that many suffer. He gave the church servants who are primarily responsible to care for needs among the body of Christ. God is not creating an unnecessary dichotomy of care but recognizing whole person care within the life of the church. Deacons are to work in tandem with the elders, not as separate entities. The responsibility of deacons is not exclusively physical needs that arise, and neither is the responsibility of elders exclusively spiritual needs. The primary focus of each office demonstrates God's intention for his church to care deeply and specifically for the needs of his people. Deacons were instituted to defend the vitality and importance of the ministry of the Word and prayer. This is what remains central for growing faith and faithfulness in the church.

Response of God's Flock to the Care of Under-Shepherds

Sheep were intended to be shepherded. We are governed by Christ; we are a priesthood of believers with Christ as our shepherd. Yet, God ordained his church to have overseers with responsibilities to "keep watch" over us.

Our default position should be respect and submission to those in oversight of us. To reiterate, this does not mean unthinking obedience in the same way that overseers do not have unbridled authority. One of the ways we obey Christ and honor him is to honor those in authority over us. As with every other legitimate, delegated authority on earth, we are to obey in the Lord. We are to remain as Bereans, testing everything we hear against the Word of God revealed in Scripture (Acts 17:10–12). Our response to our elders who are in authority over us generally reflects our heart disposition before our supreme authority, God.

Based upon Hebrews 13:17, if elders are to *keep watch* over our souls, then we should be vulnerable enough to allow them to know the state of our soul. Being known by our elders allows them to speak the Word of God more specifically to us as we continue to grow. We should also have a posture toward them that allows admonishment or exhortation when necessary as well as encouragement and edification. As Christians, it's important to maintain a heart of humility toward elders because God has given them to us as a primary means to care for our soul.

Conclusion

As mentioned earlier, when pastors hear teaching on biblical counseling they often raise a concern of burnout with the responsibilities they already carry. This is why it is important to reshape our view of "professionalized" pastoral ministry. While pastors should be leading and modeling this type of ministry among their people, every Christian is called to minister to each other and bear the burdens of one another as we are conformed to the image of Christ.

How does that happen? The elders, under-shepherds called by Christ, are entrusted with equipping the saints for the work of the ministry. This is one primary way to build a culture of care in your church. The next chapter will unpack how that can happen.

Discussion Questions

1. How has the professionalization of pastoral ministry impacted both pastors and church members? How has it impacted your church?
2. What are some ways that elders are called to "keep watch" and "pay careful attention" to the sheep in their care?
3. What is the role of the Spirit and the Word in under-shepherding?
4. What should the relationship be between public and personal ministry in the church? How is your church doing in these areas?

CHAPTER SEVEN

Equipping the Saints

The weight and responsibility of pastoral ministry can be overwhelming. When pastors hear about biblical counseling, many agree with the basic principles of the sufficiency of Scripture and the work of the Spirit to heal the wounded soul. However, even after a pastor is convinced of the need for personal ministry of the Word, questions arise regarding its practice.

Most pastors are busy with a wide range of responsibilities. Pressures mount as pastors consider the time involved in personal ministry of the Word along with their other pastoral duties. "How in the world will I have time to invest personally in counseling hours," he might ask, "if I am going to properly prepare for a sermon each week?" Others might wonder, "If I am responsible for counseling and soul care it seems that is all I would do in a week's time." All he sees is more exhaustion in his future if he pursues personal ministry of the Word, fulfilling his duty as shepherd to keep watch over the souls of his flock.

Those are fair concerns for the pastor if he is alone in the task, but he is forgetting that God has also called the whole church to care for each other. While pastors have been given the primary responsibility to care for souls, caring for individuals is the work of the church as a whole. Shepherding care is to be a weight shared by elders. As we saw in the previous chapter, elders are responsible to keep watch over the souls of the flock of God among them and to ensure that any needs they identify are being met. Deacons, as we also discussed, are to help relieve pressure on the elders by caring for the needs of members, especially those that are of a physical nature. But the work of the ministry is not limited to these two offices.

Paul reminds us in Ephesians 4:12 that the leaders in the church are to be equipping the saints for their work in the ministry. He says elsewhere that it is the responsibility of all believers to be ministers of reconciliation (2 Corinthians 5:18–21). By God's design, Christ is the head of the church and its chief shepherd. Elders shepherd the flock of God as stewards and caretakers for Christ's sake. But every believer is called by God to minister to one another. We are each called to be the body of Christ. We are called to be his hands and feet for the sake of each other. We are called to minister his Word as his counsel for encouragement, comfort, correction, discipline, and so much more.

Paul urges we who are in Christ to "*walk* in a manner worthy" of our calling (Ephesians 4:1, emphasis added). He reiterates his urging, in verse 17, to *walk* not as unbelievers in the "futility of their minds." Our walk is the way we live life. It is the putting on of the life in Christ and the putting off of our old nature. He finishes the chapter with practical examples of how we should strive to grow in grace by putting on our new life. Practice and doctrine are never intended to be separate. Biblical doctrine always demands practice, and our practice is always to be rooted in sound doctrine. Revelation is intended to elicit our response in worship and honor to God in all things (Colossians 3:16–17).

In between Paul's exhortations regarding how we should live according to the way we have learned Christ, he provides further instruction on how we learn to walk. He addresses us as individuals, but never to the exclusion of our important and collective work as the body of Christ. The church is central to the function of our ability to walk faithfully. The reason is because the church is the ground and pillar of the truth (1 Timothy 3:15). It is the truth that sanctifies us, sets us free, and readies us for every good work (John 17:17; 2 Timothy 3:17). But that is not all it does. The church is the steward of this truth, and the functions of the body of Christ serve to build us up for this work of the ministry.

Those who serve the church in the role of elder have a particular purpose. As they keep watch over souls, they are to actively equip the saints for the work of the ministry. Saints are to be equipped to serve the church by ministering the word of God for the care of souls. By "the care of souls" I mean working by the power of the Holy Spirit, utilizing his sword to bring both justification and sanctification to the hearts of people. This work of the ministry is doing the work of Christ to build up his body.

The Goal: Maturity in Christ

The aim of unity in faith and knowledge in the body is that we all become mature in Christ. The attainment of the stature of Christ does not happen by any other means than the work of the church in the ministry of the Word, by the power of the Holy Spirit. When we are built up to maturity in Christ, we are not immune from suffering, but we become most fully human. It is in the image of Christ that we most reflect the purposes for which man was created. It is in the image of Christ that we are most healthy and stable. When we lack wisdom from God, which can only be found in Christ, we live double-souled lives, unstable (disordered) in all of our ways (James 1:2–8).

It is no wonder that the world's way of describing mental vexations is as disorders. They are human expressions of an unstable life in terms of behaviors, thoughts, and emotions. God's way of stabilizing our life does not mean we will never experience evil, difficulty, or even deep turmoil in our hearts and minds, but we can rest upon the rock of Christ who is the anchor of our souls (Matthew 7:24; Hebrews 6:19). He has chosen to care for our souls through the various functions of the church and the care of elders and deacons so that we are built up to maturity in Christ.

As the Word of God transforms our hearts, we are able to reflect the character of God. The Word of God working upon the hearts of men restores the fullness of the *imago dei*, the image of God in us. A soul is mended toward its original design to the degree that it rests upon the precepts of God. The heart then adequately reflects the character of God as a display of His glory. This is the work of Christ, mender of the brokenhearted. The Holy Spirit works in us to transform us into the image of Christ, the one who reflected— imaged—God perfectly on the earth (Colossians 1:15).

This is the way God said it would be. The redeemed are to be conformed to the image of Christ. "We are predestined," Owen affirms, "to be conformed to his image and it is this image that is produced in our souls by the power and virtue which comes from Christ."[1] Jesus is key because he is the true human. We are to be conformed to his image, because that's the way we were designed before the corruption of sin. As Owen says, "Christ communicates himself to us by creating a new nature, his own nature, in us."[2]

Why does Christ conform us to his image? God has not changed his goal for humanity. He created us in his image, and he is transforming us from one degree of glory to another. He desires to see the earth covered with his glory, like the waters cover the sea, by forming worshippers—a people who reflect his glory (Habakkuk 2:14). This has always been God's goal for his people but is made possible by the work of Jesus.

We experience untold difficulties because of sin—our own sins, the sins of others, and the sin-cursed world we live in. Bodies decay and souls are blind. God's kindness in salvation is to heal our wounded souls, not only in our justification, but also through the sanctifying work of conforming us to the image of his Son—back to his design.

The Measure of Christ

The apostle Paul wrote that God has predestined all who are his to be "conformed to the image of his Son" (Romans 8:29). God works all things together for our good. The *good* to which he is referring is for us to be conformed to the image of Jesus.

This is the greatest good that any of us can have because, as we have discussed, Jesus is the true human. He lived as God designed man to live, worshipping God with all his heart, soul, mind, and strength while loving his neighbor. He reflected the heart of God. He reflected the character of God. Paul said of Jesus, "He is the image of the invisible God" (Colossians 1:15). He lived the way God designed humanity to live: blessed and healthy, satisfied in union with the Father. Our being conformed to his image is the plan of God because that is the way we are restored from all of the effects of sin. This transformation is consistently occurring in us until one day when we will be glorified and will "be like him" (1 John 3:2).

Until that day, God has ordained that we become like Jesus through the ministry of the Word of God in the fellowship of believers. The church is one way the Lord works all things for his glory and for our good. We gather to worship, and as we become worshipers, through the ministry of the Word and the one anothering of the body, our souls are cared for and we grow to be like Christ.

As we grow up into Christ, in his church, we are built up in love, and we are able to stand firm against evil. What a beautiful picture of care! Often we minimize the resources God has given to us for the complex work of soul care. As Jerry Bridges said, "the Word of God and prayer are two primary God-given means for building us up in the Christian faith."[3] These two means, along with work of the Holy Spirit, are often dismissed as simplistic to address the *complex problems* presented in our modern world, especially in relation to soul care. Yet I fear that we have dismissed the very things which keep us dependent upon God for help and hope. When we dismiss these God-given means, we circumvent dependence in favor of self-sustaining efforts. We embrace human wisdom, which blinds us to the beauty and excellence of the church for meaningful God-intended and God-designed care.

Truth in Love

We grow mature by being built up in Christ. Distinguished from other philosophies which seem right to our natural eyes, the way of Christ leads to strength and grace growing love from a pure heart. We are not simply growing in knowledge of any manner of subjects. We are not simply exercising our intellect to learn about people as a means of self-improvement. We are to grow up into Christ, our head! He is the aim because the goal of God-designed humanity is to love—love God and love others. We mature in Christ to guard against evil schemes. As we are built up and equipped for the ministry, we speak the truth of God's Word to others so that they may be cared for as well.

When each part of the body is growing to be like Jesus, we are equipped to speak the truth of God to each other in love (Ephesians 4:15–16). We do not simply speak truth. For truth not clothed in love bears a brutish blow to the heart and is heard by the hearer as condemnation. Nor do we simply speak in love. Love untethered to truth is no anchor for the soul. The recipe is truth in love in order to build each other up into Christ, making us strong to stand against the wiles of the evil one so that we love the broken and wounded as Christ so loved us when we were broken and wounded.

The Aim of Jesus

In previous chapters I have spent much time describing the position of Jesus as head and shepherd. I borrowed the order from Paul in Colossians as he spoke first about Jesus in his position and aim before moving on to describe the church as a reflection of the work of Christ. Paul declared some amazing truths in Colossians as he took on the heresy of Gnosticism. His key witness is Jesus as fully God and fully man. "He is the image of the invisible God," Paul said in Colossians 1:15, giving credence to the humanity of Jesus. We shouldn't miss this most critical point in the case we have been making regarding the church. Jesus is fully human, and in his humanity he reflects the image of God, the character of God.

We were created in the image and likeness of God to reflect his glory. Sin marred the image in thousands of ways—not taking away our intrinsic value as the pinnacle of God's creation, but marring our ability to reflect his character and nature. That inability manifests itself in "hostile minds"—distressed emotions, selfish thoughts, evil deeds. We can categorize this as unstable or disordered in our ways. We have need to be repaired, to be put right. But Jesus is not so. His humanity was not infected by our sin and he reflected, through his righteous life, the image of God.

The expression of the image of God in us is the most healthy and natural disposition of our humanity. Humanity cannot be fully healthy unless we are made right with God. In the proper order of things, as we are made right with God, he changes our mind, and the dispositions of our heart are at peace. This allows us to be made right with others and live quiet and peaceful lives. Our justification makes this declaration true about us in our standing before God, that we are at peace with him. It is our ongoing sanctification that allows us to experience this declarative truth lived out. The ongoing work of the Spirit in us, by the Word, helps us experience peace in a tangible way as we live out gospel truths every day.

Jesus declared his aim for us, which fits perfectly with God restoring us to stability.

> For in him all the fullness of God was pleased to dwell, and through him to reconcile to himself all things, whether on earth or in heaven, making peace by the blood of his cross.
>
> And you, who once were alienated and hostile in mind, doing evil deeds, he has now reconciled in his body of flesh by his death, in order to present you holy and blameless and above reproach before him, if indeed you continue in the faith, stable and steadfast, not shifting from the hope of the gospel that you heard, which has been proclaimed in all creation under heaven. (Colossians 1:19–23)

Jesus reconciled all things to himself by the peace offering of his blood. The peace offering to God is what reconciles us to God, changing our hostile minds and evil

behaviors. "Therefore," Paul said, "since we have been jus-
tified by faith, we have peace with God through our Lord
Jesus Christ" (Romans 5:1). Jesus's sacrifice makes us posi-
tionally right before God. But his work is not finished—he
also washes us with the water of the Word to make us holy
and blameless (Ephesians 5:26). Nothing can take away our
position as righteously clothed before God with the blood
of Christ, yet Jesus is still at work in us to make this experi-
entially true in the daily moments of our lives.

Methods of the Church

The aim of Jesus to conform his people to his image
should set the aim and methods of the church. History has
demonstrated that the church has often drifted from the central goal of proclamation and genuine fellowship. But we
cannot improve or "move on from" the work of Jesus. Paul
takes the goal Jesus gave and makes it the natural aim of the
church as a method for making people "complete" in Christ.
"Him [Jesus] we proclaim, warning everyone and teaching
everyone with all wisdom, that we may present everyone
mature in Christ" (Colossians 1:28).

The truths in this passage, as a continuation of the work
of Christ in verses 19–23, proclaimed through the church
create a distinct aim and methodology of our care. First,
we proclaim Christ. He is a nonnegotiable part of the care
of souls from a Christian perspective. It is Jesus who makes
peace; it is Jesus who *is* our peace (Ephesians 2:14). Systems of
care which deny the necessity of Christ for peace in the hearts
of mankind are presenting a different sort of "wisdom."

How do we do this? Warning and teaching are the two
broad but primary ways Paul says this is accomplished in
Colossians. Warn by the Word and teach with the Word.
This is a proclamation of the sufficiency of Scripture for the

task of the church. The task of the church is to reconcile us to God, which is how we gain peace. The church continues that work beyond justification by the same means of proclamation in order that every Christian becomes complete in Christ. It is in him that the fullness of God is pleased to dwell and the New Testament declares that is the aim for us, that we will be filled "with all the fullness of God" (Ephesians 3:19). The apostle uses the same aim here in Colossians, with slightly different language, that we make "everyone, mature in Christ."

Parents know that training children can be a difficult task. Paul often uses this metaphor to help us understand the task of making a disciple grow in maturity. I do not admonish my children if they are ignorant of my expectations. In those cases, they need to be taught. In fact, the normal disposition of our house toward our children is to teach them how to live in society in proper relationship to God. When our children are acting in ways that breach what is expected and clearly taught, we admonish. The task is exhausting, but the cumulation of constant teaching and admonishing day after day helps to produce maturity. The same arduous task is the way in which disciples are made, as we teach them to observe all that Jesus commanded (Matthew 28:18–20).

The church proclaims by warning and teaching so that God's people may walk by faith. In Colossians 2:6, Paul reminds us, "as you received Christ Jesus the Lord, so walk in him." We are made complete in Christ by the public and private proclamation of God's Word which leads to faith (Romans 10:17). Faith in Christ destroys the hostility in our minds. Faith in Christ mortifies sin which so easily entangles. Faith in Christ brings rest to our souls because he is our peace. The aim of Jesus helps to set the course of the function of the church, and it is the overflow of the ministry of the church that gives biblical counseling its vitality. This explains why conforming to the image of Christ and progressive sanctification are such critical tenets of biblical counseling. They are the means of God, in Christ, for us to be restored. The church is the steward to accomplish this work and we must remain faithful to that task.

The Expression: Worship

To equip the saints to do the work of the ministry means helping them grow in love, awe, and reverence for God, which motivates them to obey. A heart of gratitude in the work of Christ grows within us a heart of worship from which true compassion and care flow.

Our highest and grandest purpose is to become worshippers of the one true God. My deepest discontents come when my heart is not given to Christ. Moments of anger, anxiety, and fear are born from a heart that is not grateful to Christ—wanting my own way, or wanting Christ's way but through my own self-serving means. Coming to God in worship cures my heart as I submit all of my desires, hopes, and frustrations to him, learning to give thanks as I do so. Praise be to God that true worshippers are not required to be perfect, but can always come to God with a contrite heart. A heart of humility is stirred and maintained as we grow in Christ.

Often we think of worship as happening almost exclusively inside a church building. True worship can and should happen there, but true worship is to be a part of our daily lives wherever we are. The everyday moments of our lives are made for worship. As our hearts are conformed more and more to Christ, we see that worship becomes the constant disposition and glorious opportunity of our days. When we comfort another or bear the burdens of others, we are worshipping God by reflecting his character in the lives of the needy. When we serve others, we are reflecting the heart of our Savior which is an act of worship. God is constantly giving us opportunities to transform the mundane moments of life into life-giving acts of worship. When we forgive others for legitimate offenses against us, that is worship. Whether we exhort or sing, whether we show hospitality or admonish, whether we teach or rejoice, to do all of this in love for God is to worship him. Living in this way for the glory of God is life to us. It's becoming what the Father has been seeking all along—those who worship him in spirit and in truth (John 4:23).

The Expression: Personal Holiness

The call to personal holiness is a key component of the Lord's work in the church. The end goal of personal holiness is Christlikeness, not pharisaical hypocrisy. A concern that many have about the pursuit of holiness is that it can result in pride. But true holiness results in humility and compassionate. Paul says that the result of putting on Christ is "compassionate hearts, kindness, humility, meekness, and patience, bearing with one another" (Colossians 3:12–13). Holiness builds into our hearts a dependence upon God for our own needs and a tenderness that moves outward to care for others. The only way to care for others like Christ is to be conformed to the image of Christ.

Don't miss the important function of the body here. The church, as mentioned in the previous chapter, is to proclaim Christ so that every Christian is complete, built up in Christ. God has given the church and the means he provides her so that each member of the body grows. We begin to grow selfless as the Spirit builds compassion, kindness, and humility to bear one another's burdens into each of us.

As we are conformed to the image of Christ, we see people differently. We notice their burdens and want to help bear them. We seem to think Jesus *needs* us to work like Martha in order for his kingdom to come, when what Jesus wants is the heart of passion and love found in Mary. Our busyness, even about Christian things, can be distractions from Christ. The doing of good things is not the ultimate goal, but the gaining of Christ. The posture of Mary, to sit in humility at the feet of Jesus with ears tuned to him, is needed (Luke 10:38–42).

The pursuit of holiness is intended to happen within the context of the local body. The relationships we keep in the life of our church community are the testing grounds for how the Word is dwelling within us. Everything the church does in ministry of the Word is to deeply affect me personally, so that I grow in ministering with compassion toward others. This is not a linear process where you arrive at holiness and no longer need to grow. You don't need to achieve a particular level of holiness in order to minister to the needs of others. This is a fluid, organic process that happens as we sit under the Word continually in the fellowship of others. As we grow in the Word, a natural overflow is ministry to others. We minister to the needs of others and receive ministry from others in the same heart. This fluid process is what makes the life of the body vibrant as God's people orbit around the ministry of the Word.

The Expression: Care for One Another

The church, Francis Schaeffer said, "must be more than merely a preaching point and an activity generator; it must show a sense of community."[4] The church does need the centrality of the Word, demonstrated by the faithful proclamation of the Word week after week. But there must be intentionality to live out the Word through relationships within the household of faith. I think this is one of the reasons the New Testament epistles were written largely to the gathered people of God. It is in the context of the local body that the Word of Christ is practiced for the glory of God, the crucifying of our natural inclinations, and the good of our brothers and sisters. "One who wants more than what Christ has established," Bonhoeffer said, "does not want Christian brotherhood. He is looking for some extraordinary social experience which he has not found elsewhere; he is bringing muddled and impure desires to Christian brotherhood."[5]

True community in the family of God is a unity that is maintained around the truth of God's Word. Bonhoeffer again states, "The basis of the community of the Spirit is truth."[6] Our ministry of care and discipleship is an individual and congregational pursuit at conforming to Christ. The "one anothers" are the methodological ways God reveals the application of truths to our own heart and to the hearts of others. They are the muscles that give animation and movement to the skeletal structure of the teaching of the Word. All of this happens, of course, as the Spirit gives understanding, conviction, and strength to obey.

The "one anothers" in the Bible are specific ways God has given us to be cared for and to care for others. Several of them have a teaching component. We are to teach and admonish, instruct, speak truthfully in love, encourage, build up, and stir up *one another*. Other responsibilities we have are to give direct care to each other. We care by comforting, bearing burdens, serving, being hospitable, pursuing genuine fellowship, and seeking the good of *one another*. We are also called to maintain the unity that has been given to us by the Spirit so that we live at peace with all as far as it depends on us. We do this by forgiving, bearing with, not grumbling or speaking against, and seeking to be at peace with *one another*. These commands are active pursuits of the ministry of soul care. The brilliant part of God's design is that to obey these commands we must die to self and be conformed to his image. Then, as we grow in maturity and reflection of his character, we are also growing in giving intentional care for the good of others.

Conclusion

The church is the body of Christ. Being part of his body is not simply attending a scheduled service, listening to faithful preaching, and placing our name on a membership roll. We are the body of Christ because we are a redeemed people. We have been reconciled to God, and we are one in Christ. As a body we are members of one another, called to care for each other. As the body of Christ we comfort, serve, bear burdens, exhort, forgive, sing, show hospitality, rejoice, admonish, pray, teach, commit, encourage, help, and speak the truth in love. We do all of this in ways that are beautiful, difficult, sacrificial, and countercultural. We care for souls because God gave us his church to be his community of care, his Word as our guide for care, and his Spirit as the strength of our care. As pastors lead and members serve, God builds a renewed and unified community in the midst of a broken world. We do not need to fear our responsibility or neglect our calling. Rather, we pursue this eternally valuable act of being the church, and as we do we become a culture of care. But this type of care and this type of community takes every member of the body.

All of us are messy. We vacillate between being not nearly as good as we think we are to not nearly as bad as we know we could be. A baseline truth about the church is that none of us are perfect and we all need to grow and change. It is amazing how God designed such a gathering of imperfect people, led by a perfect Savior, with a sufficient Word, and guided by the Holy Spirit. The church is a place where despite our frailties and inadequacies we can care and be cared for; we can be served and serve; we can be corrected and correct; we can grow and help others to grow. There should be no passive bystanders in the church. Rosaria Butterfield captures this idea in her book *The Gospel Comes with a House Key*:

> Sometimes I play the posture of host, obeying God's commands, and sometimes I am in the role of guest, receiving nourishment and care. But we are always one or the other—we are either hosts, or we are guests. The Christian life makes no room for independent agents, onlookers, renters. We who are washed in the blood of Christ are stakeholders. . . . We are hosts and guests together, and both generous giving and open receiving bless God.[7]

In God commanding us to meet the needs of others, he strategically created a family of people to take care of us. When we pour ourselves out for others, as the gospel demands of us, others are called to do the same unselfishly toward us. God grows us and yet cares for us, all at the same time.

Discussion Questions

1. Why is "equipping the saints" a key task for elders?
2. What resources has God provided for equipping others? Why might we be tempted to dismiss them as insufficient?
3. How does learning to worship as part of daily life equip the saints?
4. How "holy" must someone be before they start caring for others?

CHAPTER EIGHT

Counseling in the Local Church

Although counseling is included within the category of "care for one another," this final chapter will be devoted to examining it more closely, since it is one of the primary forms of soul care that the modern American church seems to be abandoning its responsibility to provide. In theory we want to be a part of a church body where there is a culture of care. We desire obedience to the "one anothers" of Scripture. They provide a sense of belonging and are the normal processes by which care within the church should be given. But what happens in the church when specific problems arise? How do we help someone who seems overwhelmed with fear or anxiety? What about those who are struggling with sinful destructive patterns? What about those times when difficult trials and grief threaten to overwhelm? Those moments take more intention and focused care beyond the normal patterns of the "one anothers." By that, I do not mean something entirely different, but a more intensive focus and intentional application of the "one anothers."

Counseling care is a relationship with an intensive focus on an acute problem where specific attention is given toward a restorative solution. The goal of life, according to biblical truth, is to glorify God. That goal does not change for believers, even when the most devastating effects of our fallen world impact life. The church, because we have been given the Word, the Spirit, and one another is best positioned and equipped in God's economy to address these types of counseling issues.

Counseling is happening all of the time within the church, most often informally. More formal counseling relationships incorporate a person who has an identifiable problem, is intentionally pursuing help, and clear biblical solutions are being sought with the help of another believer. The natural overflow of "one another" ministry is the engagement of more intensive and directive discipleship as acute problems arise within the church body. Naturally, more mature believers will be sought out for help and be watching out for other believers in need.

There are many reasons a church may not give their attention to counseling and soul care. One may be that there is not a healthy culture of care within the church. Another is that the "one anothers" are not consistently practiced or encouraged. Another still is that the church does not see itself as the entity responsible for the care of souls. The cumulative effect is a coldness in relationships and superficial fellowship among the body of Christ. The culture of the church is not rooted in love for one another as Jesus commanded. Devoted disciples are not the mark of a church that lacks a true culture of care.

Are All Counselors?

Every believer is a counselor. By that I do not mean every believer is called or qualified to do formal counseling with individuals struggling with very difficult forms of sin and suffering. However, I do mean that every believer is to be engaged in the care of souls within the body of Christ, and as such they will provide "counsel" or wisdom for living during the course of their normal conversations. Every member of the body is called to minister the Word to one another. Everyone gives counsel—some counsel may be good, and some may be bad, but everyone gives counsel. We offer it in our gestures, by our attention, in our attitudes, by our behaviors, and with our words. We must grow in our awareness of the ways in which we already offer counsel to others and receive it from them so that we can be intentional about our relationships.

What type of counselor are you? Is your counsel shallow? Is it dominated by cultural ideas or fads? Or do you give counsel that is based on the wisdom of the Wonderful Counselor? Everything we think, say, and do makes a statement about God. Are the things you think, say, and do in your interactions with others accurate representations of the character of God?

God has intended that his Word dwell so richly in his people that we are able to counsel one another from his wisdom. Of course, we fall short, but the Spirit guides and, along with the Word, corrects us in our errors and encourages us to persevere in pursuing growth. We should intentionally aim to have our conversations always reflect the wisdom of God and how he sees the world. We will understand our lives much better and be able to offer meaningful wisdom to others as they journey through life.

With this understanding of counseling as being part of normal church life, I would like to examine two primary purposes of counseling and explore some ways in which this kind of discipleship care can be carried out within the church.

Preventative Care

Our human efforts to insulate ourselves from the difficulties and troubles of life have an appearance of wisdom but are "powerless" to protect and are of "no value" in stopping the flesh (Colossians 2:23). It is the ministry of the Word which equips us to grow and to become stable and sturdy. The Word works as preventative care for our souls. This is what Jesus says in Matthew 7:24–27—if we hear his words and do them, then we will be stable, like being firm on a rock despite the raging storms. But those who hear Jesus's words without putting them into practice will be like someone building their life on the sand. The implication is that the life not built on Christ and his Word will feel out of control or remain at the mercy of circumstances. When we are not equipped by the teaching of the Word in the fellowship of other believers, we are susceptible to human wisdom and deceitful schemes of the evil one.

Paul warned the Colossian believers not to be taken "captive by philosophy and empty deceit" (Colossians 2:8). The word of caution is to guard our hearts and minds with all vigilance, consistent with Proverbs 4. In 2 Corinthians 10:5, Paul encourages us to "take every thought captive," and in Philippians to think on things that are true (Philippians 4:8). These statements express the same truth in both its positive and negative form. He wants Christ's followers to think about some things and to avoid thinking about others. The reason is that our thoughts affirm or squelch our affections. Dwelling on biblically true things helps to affirm what God loves and to turn from our own selfish desires. The mind that does not take captive worldly ideas will affirm and rationalize our self-centered desires and suppress the truth.

Paul knew the capability of the human heart to chase after the worldly wisdom that leads to the tossing of our hearts to and fro. Our hearts have a natural appetite for soothing our longings with the wisdom of the world. But the castle walls of our heart are protected when the truth of

Christ stands guard at our heart (Philippians 4:7). Yet, how foolish we are to welcome the earthly thoughts—deceitful schemes and human wisdom—behind the walls and into the courts of our heart and mind. We let the enemy in, unsuspecting, and then we walk no longer by faith but by trust in the wisdom born from below. Our hope rests, then, on corruptible things and temporary pleasures. The result is that the walls of our hearts and minds are breached, and we waver under a burdened conscience.

Because of our human tendency to wander from scriptural truth, our souls require constant care. God has graciously granted a means of preventative care for us in the function of the church shepherds to equip us for the work of the ministry. As we are built up into the full measure of Christ, we are becoming mature and stable ready to stand firm despite the storms of life. Teaching the truth to one another, the church "inoculates" believers so they can quickly recognize and overcome the "foreign invaders"— deceptive thoughts of earthly wisdom. By this I do not mean that believers become immune to difficulty or hardship. The Word raises our awareness of deceptive patterns of unbiblical thinking and provides eyes to see and hope to persevere so that we are not put to shame (Romans 5:5). Regularly hearing the Word and participating in fellowship with one another keeps us vigilant and keenly aware of unbiblical thinking that binds or blinds the mind. Yes, an ounce of prevention can be worth a pound of cure (Proverbs 4:23).

Preventative care should be a normal part of the one-anothering life of the church. Elders share truth with church members. Brothers and sisters learn to share biblical truth with one another. This type of care should happen informally at church through conversations, small groups, hospitality, and mentoring.

But what happens when we fail? Preventive methods of teaching and discipleship in the church are primary methods of proper care. Our primary foes—the world, the flesh, and the devil—are formidable and are quite cunning. There will be moments for believers, even the most mature, when we succumb to sinful thinking or when suffering makes us weary and unstable (James 1:2–8). These difficult moments of life call for more intensive care. They should not be defined, however, in worldly terms and deferred away from biblical care. Intensive care requires more immediate attention. Formal counseling, or intensive discipleship, is that focused care which imitates leaving the ninety-nine to care for the one (Matthew 18:7–14).

Intensive Care

Formal counseling is not ministry that should be offered as one option among many—like choosing your own dish from a restaurant menu. Having a formal counseling ministry, as good as that may be, does not create a culture of care. Quite the opposite is true. Formal counseling ministries, if not guarded intentionally by the church, can be viewed as the only place where care is given in the church. As I mentioned above, the normal process is preventative care through the "one anothers," while formal counseling ministry is more like the involvement of a specialist for a deeper look into acute issues. General practitioners see the bulk of patients in their practice of medicine. Specialists are called upon for specific purposes for a more intense look at an issue, but they are not intended to replace the normal care of prevention and treatment provided by the general practitioner. Similarly, formal counseling ministry is not intended to subvert or deter normal care within the body of Christ. It is to be offered when an acute problem is identified that needs devoted attention.

Having a thriving pulpit ministry and a culture of discipleship that breeds love for one another in obedience to the commands of Jesus overflows toward healthy one-on-one counseling. This organically grown atmosphere leads very naturally into a formal counseling ministry, but it is the overflow of healthy biblical discipling and caring relationships that creates a demand for a more formal counseling ministry. When the church is known as a place of biblical love and care, people are comfortable to seek help. A formal counseling ministry is able to thrive when a church has a culture of care. Formal counseling should always have the goal of counselees moving back into the normal processes of care and growth within the church. A formal counseling ministry should always be trying to work itself out of a job. The ministry should not create people who are dependent upon the formal counseling process long-term. The goal is for intensive care to move our dependence back upon Christ through the normal means of care provided by church fellowship around the Word of God.

Formal counseling ministry is the overflow of the church's normal responsibility to care as we are empowered by God and his provision of resources for the task. Proper soul care is not primarily found in a lecture or formal teaching but is embodied in human relationships centered upon the sufficient Word of God, empowered and unified by the Spirit of God.

When a church does not intentionally practice the "one anothers" of Scripture it reveals a lack of love for one another. It is the love of Christ that *controls* or *compels* believers to live sacrificially for the sake of others (2 Corinthians 5:14). The love of Christ which animates our hearts to display his genuine care for others is stirred by the ministry of the Word. The ministry of the Word in the church not only equips, it motivates our compassion and care to love others because it is in Scripture we learn of Christ's first and forever love toward us. The "one anothers" are not simply manufactured by duty in the church but are motivated by delight from hearts that are keenly aware of the deep love of Christ for them. As the love of Christ transforms our hearts it informs and instructs our care for others.

When the church abdicates its responsibility to care for souls, it is such a detriment to the vitality of the body of Christ. We experience God's power at work in his church as we embrace and embody the heart of Christ—full of gentleness, care, and compassion. We witness the Lord's power in changing and redeeming broken lives who are living testaments to his kindness.

Living Testaments

My desk at home has a few drawers filled with letters, cards, and pictures from individuals and families I have counseled over the years. Each of them represents a story of God's grace and power to restore and redeem. As Paul reminds the church in Corinth, "You yourselves are our letter of recommendation, written on our hearts, to be known and read by all. And you show that you are a letter from Christ delivered by us, written not with ink but with the Spirit of the living God, not on tablets of stone but on tablets of human hearts" (2 Corinthians 3:2–3). The stories are actual demonstrations of God's actions toward his people. They display the character of our God before the church so that the church may remember and rejoice. The stories act, in many ways, as stones of remembrance.

You may recall when Samuel "took a stone and set it up between Mizpah and Shen and called its name Ebenezer; for

he said, 'Till now the LORD has helped us'" (1 Samuel 7:12).
Joshua did something similar years before when the children
of Israel crossed the Jordan. Joshua appointed one man from
each of the tribes to gather a stone from the riverbed where
the priests marched over with the ark. He said to them,

> Pass on before the ark of the LORD your God into
> the midst of the Jordan and take up each of you a
> stone upon his shoulder, according to the number of
> the tribes of the people of Israel, that his may be a
> sign among you. When your children ask in time to
> come, "What do those stones mean to you?" then
> you shall tell them that the waters of the Jordan were
> cut off before the ark of the covenant of the Lord.
> When it passed over the Jordan, the waters of the
> Jordan were cut off. So these stones shall be to the
> people of Israel a memorial forever. (Joshua 4:5–7)

So an Ebenezer is a marker by which we remember God's
lovingkindness, as the one who restores the brokenhearted.

So what stories are crammed in my overflowing desk
drawers? They are all stories of how God changed people
using his Word and his church. A few of the stories come
directly from my personal counseling ministry, but it was not
me that was the main conduit of care—it was our church.
One example is a family from a witness protection program
who landed in our small town and somehow in our small
church. They were vulnerable and naturally afraid due to
the unfolding of events from their past. As laughter replaced
tears and their flourishing relationships in the church
replaced their seclusion and solitude, the name of Christ
was exalted. They began to trust in the promises of God
rather than believe that their terrible past circumstances

determined their future. Their hearts were settled, and the joy of their lives was a vivid testimony of God's providential care to our church body.

In that same drawer is a family photo. I never met the majority of the family, but one day the wife in the photo walked into our church office. She was from another church in our community but had been referred to our counseling ministry by one of our church members. She sat in my office with the lady who referred her. As tears were streaming down her face, she confessed she was ready to leave her husband. She doubted if he was a believer because of his lack of interest in church or the things of God, even though he had professed Christ earlier in life. We met on two different occasions, and I simply tried to encourage her. She diligently completed the few bits of homework I gave. She continued to speak with the friend who referred her to receive encouragement and prayer, and we did not meet again for counseling after the second appointment.

About six or eight months later, I was in my office studying when the church secretary knocked on my door to say that someone wanted to see me for a minute. Quite surprisingly, the same lady peeked her head around the corner of my office door. She said that she only had a minute but wanted to give me something. She handed me the photo of her family, and with tears of joy in her eyes she explained how the Lord had saved her husband. She wanted to give me this family picture to say thank you because, as she put it, "this photo would not have been possible without your godly counsel." My godly counsel would not have been possible without a church member who cared deeply for her and wanted to walk with her through those very dark days of her life. What a testimony to God's faithfulness! And there are many more stories to be told that are not written in letters of thanks with ink, but more in lives that have been restored as a wonderful testimony of God's power and faithfulness to display his character and encourage his church.

A More Excellent Way

What if we were keenly aware of the depth of our own neediness? What if we embraced our weaknesses? What if we relished in our dependence upon our Savior? What if we created a culture in our church that was not based on piety too high to obtain, but the reality that we are all being conformed to the image of Christ? The Word would be central and the work of the Spirit necessary. Our humility would flourish, and the grace of Christ would flow freely from us. The broken would find refuge in the same way that we all have found refuge in our Lord's mercy. Biblical doctrine would be foundational and uncompromising, because we would all understand that our lives depend on knowing the truth of who God is.

The triune God of the Bible is the only independent being. He needs nothing to subsist. While we act as if we are independent and our culture pretends we are, the reality is, we are all dependent. As we come to grips with that reality, the taste of the Word becomes sweeter. Our confidence in its wisdom is less academic or intellectual and more experiential as we trust in the sweet name of Jesus for our stability. That sense of weakness would establish our hope in the strength of our strong Savior.

When we embrace our weaknesses and find sustaining grace in Christ, we better engage the weaknesses of others with humility, compassion, and grace. Every time I find some wonderful eatery, I brag to others about the sweets and savories. How much more will we boast in our Lord, his Word, and the fellowship of his people when we find strength, encouragement, and correction as we wrestle with our own frailties. The sweetness of his Word is our delight, and we hold dear the wholesome fellowship and prize it above earthly treasures.

Our weaknesses must be described in biblical ways. Continuing to categorize our problems by the world's subjective systems only exacerbates the stigma within the church. Reclaiming a biblical understanding of our very real problems provides us with a means toward hope. Now the church can minister well without fear—unafraid to grow and unafraid to engage the most broken lives—because we know the life-giving work of God among the body of Christ for the "least of these." He sustains us daily by his grace and mercy, and he will not withhold his abundant mercy to the contrite in spirit. He will sustain and strengthen, and we are confident of this because he continues to demonstrate himself faithful to each of us.

One final thought—the body of Christ must create an atmosphere where it is okay to ask for help. It is okay to admit weakness. We must be unafraid to get help ourselves from the body of Christ. We are often willing to give care to others who are in need, but can easily neglect to seek care when we ourselves are in need. Unintentionally we create a barrier between the truly *needy* and ourselves—the ones who seem to have it all together. The church then creates an atmosphere which communicates that some people are above needing care. The result is that believers remain at arm's length from each other, hesitant to be transparent when in need. The point is that we all need help; we all need constant care and oversight of our souls. The culture in the church must reflect the heart of our own neediness and dependence upon Christ. This is what the desperate find so attractive in a church family. We then gain a reputation outside that we truly love one another—and people feel welcomed by that humility, confident that this is a place where they can find refuge, hope, and love.

Erasing the Stigma

The only way we can erase the stigmas associated with our human frailty is to build a culture of care. A church where the DNA is centered around the ministry of the Word in the functions prescribed by the Word in the power of the Spirit. Our care supersedes talk therapy and professionalized counseling ministry, because it is whole-life care. The care of the church is multifaceted because it is intended to span the depths of our experiences woven through the moments of our lives. The care is not limited to a fifty-minute counseling session. The harmony of exhortation, admonition, encouragement, forgiveness, teaching, prayer, love, worship, and a host of other "one anothers" fights against the stigma to offer genuine care. It meets people where they are but doesn't leave them there.

We do not ostracize the weak—we help them. We do not condone the prideful—we admonish them. We do not avoid the weary—we encourage them. We do not neglect the needy—we give as anyone has need. The stigma that is attached to our problems crumbles against the genuine care of the church.

Stigmas will remain if we do not reclaim biblical categories of human suffering and sin from the grips of humanistic social scientists. God has given us exactly what we need to care appropriately in the moment. We do all of this with the tools God has given to demonstrate the beauties of Christ— the hope of the world. We sacrifice counterculturally, because God has given the church as his community of care, his Word as our guide for care, and the Holy Spirit as the empower-ment of our care. Individually we strive to grow a harmony of messy relationships so that we love God in unity and then love others with the love with which he has loved us.

We will never do all of this perfectly. Our failures are a constant reminder of our shared dependence upon Jesus. We must be quick to repent in our failures, quick to embrace our weaknesses, and quick to seek the help from our family in Christ during our times of need. A church that dwells richly in the Word keeps hearts tender toward God in personal repentance and tender toward others to remain keenly aware of their burdens. A heart constantly warmed by God's Word and encouraged by his people strengthens our spiritual backs to bear the burdens of others with grace and longsuffering. That spiritual fortitude to bear burdens is not found in any other source.

The world needs a church that cares well. Our ability to bear burdens and walk in love with one another will make more apologetic impact than even the most well-reasoned and true arguments against secular philosophies of care. May elders strive to shepherd and equip the flock of God to maturity as they view growth in Christ and security of peace with God as the true means of health for the inner man. May we strive with all of our energy, as Paul, to make each other complete in Christ. May we love one another with an unwavering commitment which displays we are true disciples of Christ. As we grow, we will not need to manufacture systems of care, but simply be the church that displays the glorious character of the Lord Jesus for the oppressed, wounded, broken, and lost. May we strive with all that is in us to be the church as God designed to show his heart of care in our love and deeds to the wounded in heart.

We must remember that our aim is love. We may be the most skilled and discerning counselors in the world, but if we are not fostering love of God and love of others in our own lives and in the lives we counsel, then we are a clanging symbol (1 Corinthians 13:1). The end of soul care in the church is to glorify God by loving others, which displays that we are true disciples of Christ. Our hearts are set on another world, as we proclaim this world is broken, but Jesus is coming to make all things new. The means by which we obtain this aim and care is the love of Christ Jesus. Remember, we love because he first loved. Soul care ministry in the church begins and ends with Jesus, the great redeemer and restorer of our souls. "The law of the LORD is perfect, reviving the soul" (Psalm 19:7).

One day there will be no need for counseling ministry. Jesus will come and make all things new (Revelation 21:5). If he is the source of our hope then to make all things new, then he is the source of our hope and peace now and we will patiently await his coming, dependent upon his promises. The church is the ground and pillar of this truth and, until he comes, will remain the institution God designed to care for souls.

Discussion Questions

1. Do you think of yourself as a counselor? Why or why not?
2. How does offering preventative soul care help when intensive care is needed?
3. What should the culture of the church that offers intensive care look like? How is that different than the model of care in our culture?
4. The last part of this chapter describes a church culture of dependence on God and each other, where people with problems are not stigmatized but instead offered help. How can your church grow in becoming this kind of culture?

Acknowledgments

These types of projects never reach fruition without significant collaboration and encouragement. The staff at New Growth Press has been patient with constant delays from me, yet resilient in expediting the process once the manuscript was in their hands. The administration at Midwestern Baptist Theological Seminary have remained a consistent encouragement, and their steady support is never taken for granted.

My students are more than mere learners but are contributors as they stimulate my thinking and continue to help me refine ideas on a myriad of subjects. Their passion to serve the church is one of the many motivations to get this work in print. My staff at ACBC is always a wonderful sounding board that spurs my thinking biblically in fear of the Lord and practically in service to his church.

The greatest debt of gratitude is owed to my family. They have borne the brunt of late nights, early mornings, and absent-minded moments as I was occupied with this project. They have all sacrificed much so that I could offer this feeble attempt to edify and exhort believers. Any praise that Jesus receives from this work, and any encouragement given to his church, you all have contributed to by your endurance and love for me through these many months of labor. Thank you, Summer, for your patience with me and for leading our children to understand sacrifice for the sake of Jesus. Daily you point us all heavenward and you are a treasure to us.

Endnotes

Chapter I

1. Jerry Bridges, *The Crisis of Caring: Recovering the Meaning of True Fellowship* (Philipsburg, NJ: P&R, 1992), 9.

2. David Powlison, *The Biblical Counseling Movement: History and Context* (Greensboro, NC: New Growth Press, 2010), 1.

3. Heath Lambert. *The Biblical Counseling Movement after Adams* (Wheaton, IL: Crossway, 2001).

4. John MacArthur, *Thinking Biblically!: Recovering a Christian Worldview* (Wheaton, IL: Crossway, 2003), 21.

5. Abraham Kuyper, *Rooted and Grounded: The Church as an Organism and Institution* (Grand Rapids, MI: Christian Library Press, 2013); Kuyper, "Sphere Sovereignty," trans. George Kamps (The Free University, October 20, 1880), https://reformationaldl. org/2019/07/17/sphere-sovereignty-abraham-kuyper; John Calvin, *The Institutes of the Christian Religion,* trans. Henry Beveridge (Peabody, MA: Hendrickson, 2008), 799–804; Rob Rienow, *Limited Church: Unlimited Kingdom* (Nashville: Randall House, 2013), 69.

6. Rienow, *Limited Church,* 61–68.

7. Francis Schaeffer, *A Christian Manifesto* (Wheaton, IL: Crossway, 1981), 19.

8. Schaeffer, *A Christian Manifesto*, 91.

9. Schaeffer, *A Christian Manifesto*, 130.

10. *ACBC Standard of Doctrine*, www.biblicalcounseling.com.

11. Jay Adams, *Competent to Counsel* (Grand Rapids, MI: Zondervan, 1986), 20.

12. Jay Adams, *A Theology of Christian Counseling* (Grand Rapids, MI: Zondervan, 1986), 279.

13. David Powlison, "Crucial Issues in Contemporary Biblical Counseling," *Journal of Biblical Counseling* (1988), 54.

14. Heath Lambert, *A Theology of Biblical Counseling: The Doctrinal Foundations of Counseling Ministry* (Grand Rapids, MI: Zondervan, 2016), 11.

15. Lambert, *Theology of Biblical Counseling*, 304. Lambert also affirmed the church by saying, "Understanding the doctrine of the church in a theology of biblical counseling is important because the church is the place where counseling ministry will most meaningfully happen. While it is important to understand theology and doctrine, we need to apply what we learn in a community of believers—in the church."

16. Mark Dever *The Church: The Gospel Made Visible* (Nashville: B&H Academic, 2012); John MacArthur, *The Master's Plan for the Church* (Chicago: Moody Publishers, 2008); Gene A. Getz, *The Measure of a Healthy Church* (Chicago: Moody Publishers, 2007).

Chapter 2

1. Anthony A. Hoekema, *Created in God's Image* (Grand Rapids. MI: William B. Eerdmans, 1994); Owen Strachan, *Reenchanting Humanity* (Fearn, UK: Christian Focus, 2019); Stephen Wellum, *God the Son Incarnate: The Doctrine of Christ* (Wheaton, IL: Crossway, 2016).

2. Mark Jones, *Knowing Christ* (Carlisle: Banner of Truth Trust, 2015), 51.

3. Lambert, *A Theology of Biblical Counseling*, 146.

4. Paul Tautges, *A Small Book for the Hurting Heart: Meditations on Loss, Grief, and Healing* (Greensboro, NC: New Growth Press, 2020); Lou Priolo, *Picking Up the Pieces: Recovering from Broken Relationships* (Phillipsburg, NJ: P&R, 2012); John Henderson, *Abuse: Finding Hope in Christ* (Phillipsburg, NJ: P&R, 2012)

Chapter 3

1. See Hannah Decker, *The Making of the DSM-III: A Diagnostic Manual's Conquest of American Psychiatry* (Oxford: Oxford University Press, 2013); and Gary Greenberg, *The Book of Woe: The DSM and the Unmaking of Psychiatry* (New York: Blue Rider Press, 2013).

2. Gary Greenberg, *The Book of Woe: The DSM and the Unmaking of Psychiatry* (New York: Blue Rider Press, 2013), 44–64; Allen Frances, *Saving Normal: An Insider's Revolt against Out-of-Control Psychiatric Diagnosis, DSM-5, Big Pharma, and the Medicalization of Ordinary Life* (New York: William Morrow, 2013), 19.

3. Frances, *Saving Normal*, 12.

4. American Psychiatric Association, *Diagnostic and Statistical Manual of Mental Disorders*, 5th ed. (*DSM-5*) (Washington, DC: American Psychiatric Association, 2013), 19.

5. *DSM-5*, 25.

6. Andrew Scull, *Psychiatry and Its Discontents* (Oakland: University of California Press, 2019); Gary Greenberg, *The Book of Woe: The DSM and the Unmaking of Psychiatry* (New York: Blue Rider Press, 2013); Anne Harrington, *Mind Fixers: Psychiatry's Troubled Search for the Biology of Mental Illness* (New York: W. W. Norton, 2019); S. Nassir Ghaemi, *The Rise and Fall of the Biopsychosocial Model: Reconciling Art and Science in Psychiatry*, (Baltimore: Johns Hopkins, 2010).

7. Joanna Moncrieff, *Myth of the Chemical Cure* (London, UK: Palgrave Macmillan, 2007); Anne Harrington, *Mind Fixers: Psychiatry's Troubled Search for the Biology of Mental Illness* (New York: W. W. Norton & Company, 2019); David Healy, *Anti-Depressant Era* (Cambridge, MA: Harvard University Press, 1999); David Healy, *The Creation of Psychopharmacology* (Cambridge, MA: Harvard University Press, 2002); Robert Whitaker, *Anatomy of an Epidemic* (New York: Crown 2010); Daniel Berger, *Rethinking Depression* (Taylors, SC: Alethia International Publications, 2019).

8. Adams, *Competent to Counsel*, xxi.

9. Nancy Pearcey and Charles B. Thaxton, *The Soul of Science: Christian Faith and Natural Philosophy* (Wheaton, IL: Crossway, 1994), 248: "science and scholarship are never carried out in a philosophical and religious vacuum." See also J.P. Moreland, *Scientism and Secularism: Learning to Respond to a Dangerous Ideology* (Wheaton, IL: Crossway, 2018), 22–41.

10. Greenberg, *The Book of Woe*; Healy, *The Anti-Depressant Era*; Moncrieff, *The Myth of the Chemical Cure*; Michael A. Taylor, *Hippocrates Cried: The Decline of American Psychiatry* (Oxford: Oxford University Press, 2013); Daniel Carlat, *Unhinged: The Trouble with Psychiatry—A Doctor's Revelations about a Profession in* Crisis (New York: Free Press, 2010); Frances, *Saving Normal*; Irving Kirsch, *The Emperor's New Drugs: Exploding the Anti-Depressant Myth* (London: The Bodley Head, 2009); Stanton Peele, *The Diseasing of America: How We Allowed Recovery Zealots and the Treatment Industry to Convince Us We Are out of Control* (Hoboken, NJ: Wiley, 1999); Whitaker, *Anatomy of an Epidemic*.

11. Francis Schaeffer, *The Church at the End of the 20th Century*, 2nd Ed. (Wheaton, IL: Crossway, 1994), 89.

12. Gerald Corey, *Theory and Practice of Counseling and Psychotherapy: The Movement toward Psychotherapy Integration*, 8th ed. (Belmont, CA: Brooks/Cole, 2009), 448.

13. Ghaemi, *Rise and Fall of the Biopsychosocial Model*; Sami Timimi, *Insane Medicine: How the Mental Health Industry Creates Damaging Treatment Traps and How You Can Avoid Them* (Self Published, 2020), 10–29; Robert Whitaker, *Mad in America: Bad Science, Bad Medicine, and the Enduring Mistreatment of the Mentally Ill* (New York: Basic Books, 2002).

14. Stanton L. Jones and Richard E. Butman, *Modern Psychotherapies*, 2nd Ed. (Downers Grove, IL: IVP Academic, 2011), 434–458.

15. Carl Trueman, *The Real Scandal of the Evangelical Mind* (Chicago: Moody Publishers, 2003), 35. See also Trueman, *The Rise and Triumph of the Modern Self: Cultural Amnesia, Expressive Individualism, and the Road to the Sexual Revolution* (Wheaton, IL: Crossway, 2020), 42–102.

16. Paolo Lionni, *The Leipzig Connection* (Sheridan, OR: Heron Books, 1993), 4.

17. David Powlison, *Seeing with New Eyes: Counseling the Human Condition through the Lens of Scripture* (Phillipsburg, NJ: P&R, 2003), 1.

18. Lambert, *A Theology of Biblical Counseling*, 38.

19. Mark Dever, *9 Marks of a Healthy Church* (Wheaton, IL: Crossway, 2013).

20. Gregory Wills, *Democratic Religion: Freedom, Authority, and Church Discipline in the Baptist South 1785–1900*, (Oxford: Oxford University Press, 2003), 10.

21. Derek Tidball, *Skillfull Shepherds: An Introduction to Pastoral Theology* (Grand Rapids, MI: Zondervan, 1986), 18–20.

22. T. Dale Johnson, Jr., *The Professionalization of Pastoral Care: The SBC's Journey from Pastoral Theology to Counseling Psychology* (Eugene, OR: Wipf & Stock, 2020), 103–130; David Wells, *No Place for Truth: Or Whatever Happened to Evangelical Theology?* (Grand Rapids, MI: Wm. B Eerdmans Publishing, 1993), 238–257.

Chapter 4

1. Elizabeth Elliot, *In the Shadow of the Almighty: The Life and Testament of Jim Elliot* (San Francisco: Harper Collins, 1989), 138–139.

2. John Owen, *The Glory of Christ* (Carlisle: The Banner of Truth Trust, 2012), 96.

3. Lambert, *A Theology of Biblical Counseling*, 137.

4. Owen, *The Glory of Christ*, 89.

5. Ed Welch, *Addictions: A Banquet in the Grave* (Philipsburg, NJ: P&R, 2001), 21.

6. David Powlison, *The Biblical Counseling Movement: History and Context* (Greensboro, NC: New Growth Press, 2010), 272.

7. Dane Ortlund, *Gentle and Lowly: The Heart of Christ for Sinners and Sufferers* (Wheaton, IL: Crossway, 2020).

8. Martin Lloyd-Jones, *Darkness and Light* (Grand Rapids, MI: Baker Books, 1982), 5.

9. Jay Adams, *Handbook of Church Discipline* (Grand Rapids, MI: Zondervan, 1986), 13.

Chapter 5

1. Thomas Oden, *Pastoral Theology: Essentials of Ministry* (San Francisco: Harper Collins, 1983), 49.

2. MacArthur, *The Master's Plan for the Church*, 73.

3. Martin Bucer, *Concerning the True Care of Souls* (Carlisle: Banner of Truth Trust, 2009), 73.

4. Owen, *The Glory of Christ*, 97.

5. Owen, *The Glory of Christ*, 89.

6. Owen, *The Glory of Christ*, 88.

7. Lambert, *Theology of Biblical Counseling*, 155.

8. This section was originally published in "Shepherds Must Bind Up the Broken," in *Pastoral Ministry: The Ministry of a Shepherd*, ed. Deron Biles (Nashville: B&H Academic, 2017), 81–100.

9. Matthew Henry, *Matthew Henry's Commentary on the Whole Bible* (Peabody, MA: Hendrickson Publishers, 2009), 1241 (Jeremiah 8:13–22).

10. Owen, *The Glory of Christ*, 97.

Chapter 6

1. Bucer, *Concerning the True Care of Souls*, 17.

2. John Piper, *Brothers We are Not Professionals: A Plea to Pastors for Radical Ministry* (Nashville: B&H, 2013); E. Brooks Holifield, *A History of Pastoral Care in America: From Salvation to Self-Realization* (Eugene, OR: Wipf & Stock, 2005).

3. Andrew Purves, *Pastoral Theology in the Classic Tradition* (Louisville: Westminster John Knox Press, 2001); Thomas Oden, *Care of Souls in the Classic Tradition* (Philadelphia: Fortress Press, 1984); Holifield, *History of Pastoral Care in America*; Tidball, *Skillfull Shepherds*; Derek Tidball, *Ministry by the Book: New Testament Patterns for Pastoral Leadership* (Downers Grove, IL: IVP Academic, 2009).

4. Alexander Strauch, *Paul's Vision for Deacons: Assisting the Elders with the Care of God's Church* (Colorado Springs: Lewis & Roth, 2017); Matt Smethurst, *Deacons: How They Serve and Strengthen the Church* (Wheaton, IL: Crossway, 2021); Tidball, *Skillfull Shepherds*; Ortlund, *Gentle and Lowly*.

5. MacArthur, *The Master's Plan for the Church*, 186.

6. Holifield, *History of Pastoral Care in America*; Piper, *Brothers We Are Not Professionals*; Johnson, *Professionalization of Pastoral Care in the SBC*.

7. Purves, *Pastoral Theology in the Classic Tradition*; Oden, *Care of Souls in the Classic Tradition*.

8. David Wells, *No Place for Truth*, 248.

9. Jeremy Pierre and Deepak Reju, *The Pastor and Counseling: The Basics of Shepherding Members in Need* (Wheaton, IL: Crossway, 2015), 30–31.

10. Bucer, *Concerning the True Care of Souls*.

11. Pierre and Reju, *The Pastor and Counseling*, 25.

12. Tidball, *Skillfull Shepherds*, 14.

13. Pierre and Reju, *The Pastor and Counseling*, 34.

14. Strauch, *Paul's Vision for Deacons*; Smetherst, *Deacons*; MacArthur, *The Master's Plan for the Church*, 90.

15. Bucer, *Concerning the True Care of Souls*, 30.

Chapter 7

1. Owen, *The Glory of Christ*, 89

2. Owen, *The Glory of Christ*, 88

3. Bridges, *The Crisis of Caring*, 13.

4. Schaeffer, *The Church at the End of the 20th Century*, 45.

5. Dietrich Bonhoeffer, *Life Together: The Classic Exploration of Christian Community* (New York: HarperCollins, 1954), 26.

6. Bonhoeffer, *Life Together*, 31.

7. Rosaria Butterfield, *The Gospel Comes with a House Key* (Wheaton, IL: Crossway, 2018), 37.

Scripture Index

Biblical Solutions for the Problems People Face

The Association of Certified Biblical Counselors is committed to championing the sufficiency of Scripture for the Church as she engages the problems people face, speaking the truth in love. Christians have the responsibility to bring the truth of God to bear on the problems of everyday life, and to embody that truth in a life of love.

At ACBC, we seek to strengthen the Church to speak the truth in love by providing a quality training and certification process, a global network of like-minded individuals and institutions, and a source of practical and biblical resources for the Church.

In short, we seek to bring *biblical solutions for the problems people face*, upholding that the method God has given to do this is *truth in love*.